A plain man's guide to

DANIEL
AND THE
REVELATION

A plain man's guide to

DANIEL
AND THE
REVELATION

ERNEST W. MARTER

First published in 1997

British Library Cataloguing in
Publication Data.
A catalogue record for this book is
available from the British Library.

ISBN 1-899505-09-01

Published by
The Stanborough Press Limited
Alma Park, Grantham, Lincolnshire
NG31 9SL, England

Contents

6

1 Jesus said we should understand

JESUS' WORDS

Jesus was warning His hearers about the destruction of Jerusalem by the Roman armies, in Matthew 24.

Note the parallel passage in Luke: *'"When you see Jerusalem surrounded by armies, then know that its desolation is near. Then let those in Judea flee to the mountains."'* (Luke 21:20, 21.)

The word *abomination* would refer to the idolatrous standards carried and worshipped by the soldiers as they would be camped around the holy city some thirty-five years after Jesus spoke these words.

Those Jews who became followers of Jesus heeded His words, and when the Governor of the Roman province of Syria, who besieged the city in AD 66, unexpectedly raised the siege, every Christian in the city took the opportunity to escape, and not one perished. The siege was renewed by Titus in AD 70. He destroyed both city and temple, and more than a million Jews perished, and a hundred thousand more were sold as slaves.

Five hundred and fifty years before the birth of Christ, when the prophet Daniel had been

MATTHEW 24:1-4, 15-16

24 Then Jesus went out and departed from the temple, and his disciples came to *him* to show him the buildings of the temple.
2 And Jesus said to them, 'Do you not see all these things? Assuredly, I say to you, not one stone shall be left here upon another, that shall not be thrown down.'
3 Now as he sat on the Mount of Olives, the disciples came to him privately, saying, 'Tell us, when will these things be? And what *will be* the sign of your coming, and of the end of the age?'
4 And Jesus answered and said to them: 'Take heed that no one deceives you.

15 'Therefore when you see the *"abomination of desolation"*, spoken of by Daniel the prophet, standing in the holy place' (whoever reads, let him understand),
16 'then let those who are in Judea flee to the mountains.'

DANIEL 9:22-27

9 And he informed *me*, and talked with me, and said, 'O Daniel, I have now come forth to give you skill to understand.
23 'At the beginning of your supplications the command went out, and I have come to tell *you*, for you *are* greatly beloved; therefore consider the matter, and understand the vision:
24 'Seventy weeks are determined
For your people and for your holy city,
To finish the transgression,
To make an end of sins,
To make reconciliation for iniquity,
To bring in everlasting righteousness,

given the prediction about the desolating abomination to fall on his home city, he had been filled with horror. Jerusalem had been destroyed by Nebuchadnezzar and was still lying in ruins, and he had at that very time been praying for its restoration.

Daniel himself had been a captive in Babylon for more than fifty years. He had been taken as a hostage with other young men related to the royal family when Nebuchadnezzar had besieged Jerusalem in 605 BC. (Dan. 1:1-7.) Other captives had been taken into exile after that, some ten thousand at one time, and eventually the city itself had been levelled in 586 BC. (2 Kings 24:14; 25:8-10.)

In the very year that Daniel and his three friends were taken to Babylon, the prophet Jeremiah had said that this desolating experience would last for seventy years. (Jer. 25:1, 11, 12.) His prediction was fulfilled twice over. Seventy years after the first captives were deported to Babylon, Cyrus of Persia, by a decree issued in 536, permitted Jews to return to Judea. (Ezra 1:1-4.) And exactly seventy years after the holy city and the beautiful temple of Solomon had been destroyed, a new temple was completed in Jerusalem in the year 516 under a decree issued by Darius Hystaspis in 520 BC. (Ezra 6:1-3, 7, 15.)

Daniel was still alive in the third year of Cyrus, but apparently did not join the returning exiles. (Dan. 10:1.) He would not have been alive when the second temple was completed, but he had the honour of being given the information by Gabriel that the city itself, for whose restoration he was so earnestly praying (Dan. 9:16-18) would indeed by rebuilt by

To seal up vision and prophecy,
And to anoint the Most Holy.
25 'Know therefore and understand,
That from the going forth of the command
To restore and build Jerusalem
Until Messiah the Prince,
There shall be seven weeks
    and sixty-two weeks;
The street shall be built again,
    and the wall,
Even in troublesome times.
26 'And after the sixty-two weeks
Messiah shall be cut off,
    but not for himself;
And the people of the prince
    who is to come
Shall destroy the city and the
    sanctuary.
The end of it *shall be* with a flood,
And till the end of the war
    desolations are determined.
27 'Then he shall confirm a covenant
    with many for one week;
But in the middle of the week
He shall bring an end to sacrifice
    and offering.
And on the wing of abominations
    shall be one who makes desolate,
Even until the consummation,
    which is determined,
Is poured out on the desolate.'

royal decree. This is the passage that Jesus encouraged his hearers to understand. It contains the prize which Daniel was seeking, and it contains even more for us.

JERUSALEM'S PROBATION EXTENDED

Daniel 9:24 '"Seventy weeks are determined for your people and for your holy city."'

'Seventy weeks' is rendered 'seventy weeks of years' by the RSV, and 'seventy times seven years' by the REB. Gabriel will tell Daniel what will happen in this period of 490 years. Daniel had confessed that it was the sins of God's people that had brought their calamities upon them, and it is in respect to this matter of sin that Gabriel immediately began to speak.

'"To finish the transgression, to make an end of sins."'

Evidently the period of 490 years was to be given to Israel as a period of probation. A prophet who appeared later among the returned exiles clearly understood this. (Zech. 1:1-4.) This was a word of warning.

'"To make reconciliation for iniquity, to bring in everlasting righteousness."'

This was a word of hope. The Messiah, who would be 'cut off' in this period, would bring reconciliation by His substitutionary death, (Isaiah 53), and He would prove to be '"'the Lord our righteousness'"'. (Jer. 33:15, 16.)

'"To seal up vision and prophecy."'

Jesus would fulfil the Old Testament writings referring to Himself, as He must have more than once explained to His disciples. (Luke 24:26, 27, 44.)

'"And to anoint the most holy."'

The RSV and the REB render this correctly as '"the most holy place"'. This is another word of hope. It reaches beyond the calamity to fall again on the sanctuary in Jerusalem to the inauguration of Christ's priestly ministry in the sanctuary in heaven after His ascension. (Heb. 8:1, 2; Rom. 8:34; Acts 2:33.)

THE MESSIAH TO COME

25 ' "Know therefore and understand, that from the going forth of the command to restore and build Jerusalem until Messiah the Prince, there shall be seven weeks and sixty-two weeks." '

Or, as TLB puts it, ' "It will be forty-nine years plus 434 years from the time the command is given to rebuild Jerusalem, until the Anointed One comes." ' We have already seen that the decree of Cyrus in 536 directed the people to return, and that the decree of Darius succeeded in having the temple rebuilt by 516.

The people and the temple cared for, it remained for the city to be rebuilt. It was the decree of Artaxerxes Longimanus in 457, and the valiant work of Ezra and Nehemiah, that eventually achieved this result. (Ezra 7:7-11; Neh. 2:1-8.) From this date, 457 BC, Gabriel informed Daniel it would be a total of 483 years (49 plus 434) till the Messiah would appear. Ezra 7:8 indicates that it was halfway through the seventh year of Artaxerxes that the decree became effective. If then we subtract $456\frac{1}{2}$ BC years from the 483 years we get AD $26\frac{1}{2}$ years. *This gives us the date AD 27 as the year for the Messiah to appear in Israel.* And that is the very year that Jesus was 'anointed' at His baptism and began His public ministry. (Luke 3:21, 22; Acts 10:38.) No wonder the people were in expectancy when John the Baptist appeared. (Luke 3:15.) Nor should it surprise us that Jesus should begin His ministry with the words, 'The time is fulfilled.' (Mark 1:14, 15.) That Jesus was 30 years of age when He was baptized in AD 27 is due to the fact that He was not born in the year AD 1, as was thought when the Christian Era began to be used many centuries later. It is now known that Herod the Great died in the year we now count as 4 BC; Jesus was born not long before Herod died.

' "The street shall be built again, and the wall, even in troublous times." '

The troubled times of rebuilding the walls and dwellings of Jerusalem are described in Nehemiah 4:1, 6; 6:15, 16.

26 ' "And after the sixty-two weeks Messiah shall be cut off, but not for himself." '

He told His disciples plainly that when He died it would be as 'a ransom for many'. What a tragedy that the religious leaders of the people chosen by God to preserve the truth about God's covenanted plan to save mankind should have been so moved by personal envy as to engineer the death of the One through whom deliverance was to come. (Matt. 27:18; John 5:39-40.)

THE DESOLATING ABOMINATION

"And the people of the prince who is to come shall destroy the city and the sanctuary."

Titus was so impressed by the magnificence of the Jewish Temple that he gave orders that it was not to be destroyed. His orders were not obeyed by his 'people', the Roman soldiers. They had been made too desperate by the fanatical madness of the Jewish rebellion. The prophecy was literally fulfilled.

"The end of it shall be with a flood, and till the end of the war desolations are determined."

Daniel's contemporary, the prophet Jeremiah, used 'flood' to represent invading armies. (Jer. 46:7-11; 47:1-3.) A final conflict with the Romans, in the war of AD 132-135, resulted in all Jews actually being banned from the city altogether.

27 *"Then he shall confirm a covenant with many for one week."*

The last week of the seventy weeks of Jewish probation lasted from AD 27-34. For seven years the good news of the covenant of salvation was preached especially to the Jews, for three and a half years by the Saviour Himself, and after that by His followers till they were scattered abroad by severe persecution. (Acts 1:8; 8:1, 4.)

"But in the middle of the week he shall bring an end to sacrifice and offering."

At His death in the spring of AD 31, though He was being murdered by the hatred of sinful men, He 'offered Himself without spot to God', bearing our sins 'in his own body on the tree'. (Heb. 9:14; 1 Peter 2:24.) In this manner He fulfilled the typical meaning of the animal sacrifices that had been offered at the temple for hundreds of years. Thereafter the Lamb of God would take His place as both our Substitute and our Priest before the throne of God. (Rev. 5:6.) At the moment of Jesus' death the heavy veil of the temple was torn in two from the *top*. (Matt. 27:51.) In this way Heaven indicated that the divinely-ordained sacrifices had now reached their objectives and should cease.

"'And on the wing of abominations shall be one who makes desolate, even until the consummation, which is determined, is poured out on the desolate.'"

If Jesus' hearers had done what He commended — had understood the passage about the destruction of Jerusalem — they would also have discovered to their great benefit an accurate chronological prediction that plainly pointed to Himself as their Saviour. No wonder the records says: 'As he drew near, he saw the city and wept over it, saying, "If you had known . . . the things that make for your peace! . . . For the days will come upon you when your enemies will build an embankment around you . . . and they will not leave in you one stone upon another, because you did not know the *time* of your visitation."' (Luke 19:41-44.)

DANIEL UNSEALED

There are other similar predictions in the book of Daniel that have been confirmed by historical fulfilment, and there are some still awaiting fulfilment. They were written for our benefit, for the closing instructions given to Daniel were:

Daniel 12:4 *"'Daniel, shut up the words, and seal the book until the time of the end; many shall run to and fro, and knowledge shall increase.'"*

The book of Daniel is no longer sealed. Commentaries explaining it averaged about twenty each century after the Protestant Reformation. But suddenly, about AD 1800, those who loved the Word of God began to peruse Daniel's pages earnestly, running to and fro through his predictions and comparing them with the history that had occurred since he wrote. More than a hundred books about the prophecies of Daniel were published in just fifty years after 1800, and since then our 'knowledge' of his remarkable 'words' have been greatly 'increased'.

Just as it was possible for the Jews to understand the part of Daniel that applied especially to their time, so it is now possible for us who live in what Gabriel several times called 'the time of the end' to understand the divinely-given revelations that concern our own time.

REVIEW

1 When Jesus predicted that the city of Jerusalem would be destroyed, to which Old Testament prophet did He refer as evidence?

2 How must Daniel have felt about this prediction inasmuch as Jerusalem was even then in ruins on account of Israel's sins?

3 How many centuries were the Jews given as a further period of probation?

4 From what specific event were they to calculate this period?

5 Would this prophecy about the coming of the Messiah explain the general expectancy that greeted John the Baptist's mission?

6 Who tried to confirm the covenant of salvation for the first half of the last of the seventy weeks, and who proclaimed the same message for the second half of the week?

7 What was the meaning of the event that occurred in the Temple at the moment Jesus died on the cross?

8 What is the evidence that Daniel has a message not only for those times but also for us today?

DANIEL 9:24

'Seventy weeks are determind upon thy people'

(490 YEARS)	
457 BC — ORDER TO REBUILD JERUSALEM	SEVEN WEEKS 49 YEARS
408 BC — JERUSALEM REBUILT	
	SIXTY TWO WEEKS 434 YEARS
MESSIAH ANOINTED — AD 27	
MESSIAH CUT OFF — AD 31	ONE WEEK 7 YEARS
GOSPEL TO GENTILES — AD 34	

2 The successive kingdoms of men

HUMAN HISTORY

The king's dream of an image of a human being was God's revelation of '"what will be in the latter days"'. (Dan. 2:28.) The original word simply means 'the after days' or 'the later days'. In this case it extends down to our own time and deserves attention.

Daniel 2:37, 38 '*"The God of heaven has given you a kingdom .... You are this head of gold."*'

The Babylonians had in previous centuries been 'great' under Sargon I, and later under Hammurabi. After that they had for several centuries been less important than the Hittites, the Egyptians, and the Assyrians. But a new period of Babylonian glory had been inaugurated by the father of Nebuchadnezzar in 626 BC. This Neo-Babylonian Empire reached its height under Nebuchadnezzar himself. The city was not large, but it was well laid out, had massive walls, and contained the so-called hanging gardens. They were built on arches for the pleasure of his Median queen who had longed for the hills of Media. Though Babylon did not control as large an area as later empires, it was full of wealth and luxury.

DANIEL 2 and 3

2 Now in the second year of Nebuchadnezzar's reign, Nebuchadnezzar had dreams; and his spirit was *so* troubled that his sleep left him.

10 The Chaldeans answered the king, and said, 'There is not a man on earth who can tell the king's matter; therefore no king, lord, or ruler has *ever* asked such things of any magician, astrologer, or Chaldean.

11 '*It is* a difficult thing that the king requires, and there is no other who can tell it to the king except the gods, whose dwelling is not with flesh.'

12 For this reason the king was angry and very furious, and gave a command to destroy all the wise *men* of Babylon.

13 So the decree went out, and they began killing the wise *men*; and they sought Daniel and his companions, to kill *them*.

17 Then Daniel went to his house, and made the decision known to Hananiah, Mishael, and Azariah, his companions,

18 that they might seek mercies from the God of heaven concerning this secret, so that Daniel and his companions might not perish with the rest of the wise *men* of Babylon.

19 Then the secret was revealed to Daniel in a night vision. So Daniel blessed the God of heaven.

24 Therefore Daniel went to Arioch, whom the king had appointed to destroy the wise *men* of Babylon. He went and said thus to him: 'Do not destroy the wise *men* of Babylon; take me before the king, and I will tell the king the interpretation.'

27 Daniel answered in the presence of the king, and said, 'The secret which

39 *'"After you shall arise another kingdom inferior to yours."'*

Medo-Persia was a less luxurious but far more extensive empire. Soon after Nebuchadnezzar died, Cyrus, a Persian general who became son-in-law to the Median king, came to prominence in the Median Empire. It was the armies of Cyrus, named by God a hundred years before his birth as the future deliverer of Israel (Isaiah 44:24-45:4) who captured Babylon on the night of Belshazzar's feast, and placed his father-in-law, Darius, on the throne of Babylon. (Dan. 5:28-31.) About two years after that Cyrus himself became the ruler of the whole Medo-Persian Empire. Thenceforward the Persians held the place of honour. This may be observed in the reversal of the order of the names that occur in the book of Esther. (See Esther 1:3, 19.)

'"Then another, a third kingdom of bronze, which shall rule over all the earth."'

Alexander the Great conquered the whole of the Middle East, from Asia Minor and Egypt to the borders of India, in less than four years. When he arrived back in Babylon in the year 331 BC he was greeted by delegations from the West offering their submission. From that time onwards, Greek, already spoken in southern Italy, became the language of culture in Egypt,

the king has demanded, the wise *men*, the astrologers, the magicians, and the soothsayers cannot declare to the king.

28 'But there is a God in heaven who reveals secrets, and he has made known to King Nebuchadnezzar what will be in the latter days. Your dream, and the visions of our head upon your bed, were these:

29 'As for you, O king, thoughts came to your *mind while* on your bed, *about* what would come to pass after this; and he who reveals secrets has made known to you what will be.

30 'But as for me, this secret has not been revealed to me because I have more wisdom than anyone living, but for *our* sakes who make known the interpretation to the king, and that you may know the thoughts of your heart.

31 'You, O king, were watching; and behold, a great image! This great image, whose splendour *was* excellent, stood before you; and its form *was* awesome.

32 'This image's head *was* of fine gold, its chest and arms of silver, its belly and thighs of bronze,

33 'its legs of iron, its feet partly of iron and partly of clay.

34 'You watched while a stone was cut out without hands, which struck the image on its feet of iron and clay, and broke them in pieces.

35 'Then the iron, the clay, the bronze, the silver, and the gold were crushed together, and became like chaff from the summer threshing-floors; the wind carried them away so that no trace of them was found. And the stone that struck the image became a great mountain and filled the whole earth.

36 'This *is* the dream. Now we will tell the interpretation of it before the king.

37 'You, O king, *are* a king of kings. For the God of heaven has given you a kingdom, power, strength, and glory;

38 'and wherever the children of men dwell, or the beasts of the field and the birds of the heaven, he has given *them* into your hand, and has made you ruler over them all — you *are* this head of gold.

Syria and Asia Minor, as well as in Macedonia and Greece.

40 '"And the fourth kingdom shall be as strong as iron."'

Like an iron hammer working on gold, silver and bronze, the rising power of Rome was strong enough to conquer not only Macedon and Greece, Pergamum, Syria and Egypt, but also the tribes then occupying Europe. The Roman Empire never reached as far as India in the East, but it reached right across Europe to include Britain in the West. And whereas the previous three empires had each ruled for two hundred years or less, the Roman Empire ruled in the West for six centuries, and set up a system of government both at home and abroad which became a model copied in Europe for centuries afterward.

41 '"Whereas you saw the feet and toes, partly of potter's clay and partly of iron, the kingdom shall be divided."'

In the fourth and fifth centuries the European tribes took over the western Roman Empire piecemeal till the last emperor, Romulus Augustulus, decided to abdicate in AD 476. The kingdoms of Europe like to think of themselves as separate kingdoms, which indeed they always have been politically. Yet just as Egypt and Syria con-

39 'But after you shall arise another kingdom inferior to yours; then another, a third kingdom of bronze, which shall rule over all the earth.
40 'And the fourth kingdom shall be as strong as iron, inasmuch as iron breaks in pieces and shatters all *things;* and like iron that crushes, *that kingdom* will break in pieces and crush all the others.
41 'Whereas you saw the feet and toes, partly of potter's clay and partly of iron, the kingdom shall be divided; yet the strength of the iron shall be in it, just as you saw the iron mixed with ceramic clay.
42 'And *as* the toes of the feet *were* partly of iron and partly of clay, *so* the kingdom shall be partly strong and partly fragile.
43 'As you saw iron mixed with ceramic clay, they will mingle with the seed of men; but they will not adhere to one another, just as iron does not mix with clay.
44 'And in the days of these kings the God of heaven will set up a kingdom which shall never be destroyed; and the kingdom shall not be left to other people; it shall break in pieces and consume all these kingdoms, and it shall stand for ever.
45 'Inasmuch as you saw that the stone was cut out of the mountain without hands, and that it broke in pieces the iron, the bronze, the clay, the silver, and the gold — the great God has made known to the king what will come to pass after this. The dream is certain, and its interpretation is sure.'

3 Nebuchadnezzar the king made an image of gold, whose height *was* sixty cubits *and* its width six cubits. He set it up in the plain of Dura, in the province of Babylon.
2 And King Nebuchadnezzar sent *word* to gather together the satraps, the administrators, the governors, the counsellors, the treasurers, the judges, the magistrates, and all the officials of the provinces, to come to the dedi-

tinued the culture of Greece, so the European nations were in effect cultural divisions of Rome, for they inherited its language, laws and literature.

42 "'And as the toes of the feet were partly of iron and partly of clay, so the kingdom shall be partly strong and partly fragile.'"

How graphically this describes the balance of power in Europe down through the centuries. And no one has been able to bind the iron and the clay together in a permanent bond. Not Charlemagne, not Charles XII of Sweden, Charles V of Spain, Napoleon, the Kaiser, nor Hitler. And who would dare to say that a European Union could ever become anything more than a very temporary political union?

43 "'As you saw iron mixed with ceramic clay, they will mingle with the seed of men; but they will not adhere to one another.'"

Have royal intermarriages been tried, as here predicted? Why else would it be that our Prince William is descended not only from the English Alfred the Great, but also from Isabella of Spain and Fernando of Portugal, Charles the Bold of Burgundy, Charles VII of France, the Czars of Russia, Frederick of Prussia, and among others the earlier rulers of Norway, Sweden, Denmark, Saxony,

cation of the image which King Nebuchadnezzar had set up.

7 So at that time, when all the people heard the sound of the horn, flute, harp, *and* lyre, in symphony with all kinds of music, all the people, nations, and languages fell down *and* worshipped the gold image which King Nebuchadnezzar had set up.
8 Therefore at that time certain Chaldeans came forward and accused the Jews.

12 'There are certain Jews whom you have set over the affairs of the province of Babylon: Shadrach, Meshach, and Abed-Nego; these men, O king, have not paid due regard to you. They do not serve your gods or worship the gold image which you have set up.'

19 Then Nebuchadnezzar was full of fury, and the expression on his face changed towards Shadrach, Meshach, and Abed-Nego. *Therefore* he spoke and commanded that they heat the furnace seven times more than it was usually heated.
20 And he commanded certain mighty men of valour who *were* in his army to bind Shadrach, Meshach, and Abed-Nego, *and* cast *them* into the burning fiery furnace.
21 Then these men were bound in their coats, their trousers, their turbans, and their *other* garments, and were cast into the midst of the burning fiery furnace.
22 Therefore, because the king's command was urgent, and the furnace exceedingly hot, the flame of the fire killed those men who took up Shadrach, Meshach, and Abed-Nego.
23 And these three men, Shadrach, Meshach, and Abed-Nego, fell down bound into the midst of the burning fiery furnace.
24 Then King Nebuchadnezzar was astonished; and he rose in haste *and* spoke, saying to his counsellors, 'Did we not cast three men bound into the midst of the fire?' They answered and

Hungary, and Serbia? But to what avail?

44 "And in the days of these kings the God of heaven will set up a kingdom which . . . shall stand forever."

This is the happy ending of a long and not always happy story. Will it prove correct? In each particular the forecast has been correct so far. There have been only four successive empires since Daniel's time, Babylon, Persia, Greece, Rome. After that history stopped repeating. Division came, and division remains. Fifteen centuries have passed since the Roman Empire folded up, and no replacement has yet appeared. The next really significant change in history is to occur when 'a stone' will strike the image 'on its feet', and that stone will become a mountain which will fill 'the whole earth'. (Dan. 2:34, 35.) It represents the worldwide, unified, all-embracing kingdom of God. Why not take out your citizenship papers now?

said to the king, 'True, O king.'

25 'Look!' he answered, 'I see four men loose, walking in the midst of the fire; and they are not hurt, and the form of the fourth is like the Son of God.'

26 Then Nebuchadnezzar went near the mouth of the burning fiery furnace *and* spoke, saying, 'Shadrach, Meshach, and Abed-Nego, servants of the Most High God, come out, and come *here.*' Then Shadrach, Meshach, and Abed-Nego came from the midst of the fire.

27 And the satraps, administrators, governors, and the king's counsellors gathered together, and they saw these men on whose bodies the fire had no power; the hair of their head was not singed nor were their garments affected, and the smell of fire was not on them.

28 Nebuchadnezzar spoke, saying, 'Blessed be the God of Shadrach, Meshach, and Abed-Nego, who sent his Angel and delivered his servants who trusted in him, and they have frustrated the king's word, and yielded their bodies, that they should not serve nor worship any god except their own God!'

45 "The dream is certain, and its interpretation is sure."

The interpretation of this first dream in the book of Daniel is completed by the description of the coming kingdom of God in the last two chapters of the Bible. Daniel knew, was certain. Nebuchadnezzar should have known, and we may know. And we should know that the end is more important than the beginning.

HUMAN PRIDE

The golden image of Daniel 3, displayed so magnificently before the assembled leaders of the Babylonian Empire, was obviously modelled on the image which had been seen by the king in his impressive dream. The explanation of that dream had been given in answer to the earnest prayers of Daniel and these very three men. Now, as appointed administrators in local government, they were required to be present. To refuse compliance with the royal decree meant facing a horrible death in a furnace probably fired by straw soaked in the crude oil which seeped from the ground even in those days.

The king's dream had revealed to him the future course of human government and quite appropriately the revelation was presented in the form of a human being. Only the head of the image in the dream was of gold. It represented the existing empire of Nebuchadnezzar himself. The fact that the other parts of silver, bronze, iron and clay represented kingdoms which would come to power after Nebuchadnezzar was made plain, as was the fact that all of them would eventually be replaced by the eternal kingdom of God.

Nebuchadnezzar at first had been impressed by this forecast of the future, and had praised the God Daniel worshipped as '"the Lord of kings"'. (Dan. 2:47.) But evidently he had later become dissatisfied with the thought that his empire would be replaced by others. The statue he set up, completely gold-plated, was a deliberate defiance of divine revelation, and expressed his ambition that Babylon should rule forever. But this time the king would be compelled to recognize not only that God is 'a revealer of secrets', but also that '"there is no other God who can deliver"'' as God did that remarkable day. (Dan. 3:29.)

The three Jewish officials made the right decision, and as a result landed in the blazing furnace. It was so overheated that those assigned to throw them in died of the heat. But to the amazement of the king he saw the three men get up and walk around in the fire, apparently unharmed by it. In extreme agitation he called them to come out. He found them to be unhurt, having not even the smell of fire on them. After that, the rest of the day's planned proceedings were forgotten.

We shall see that this story has a stirring counterpart in the book of Revelation. Foretold there is a similar dilemma, complete with image and death decree. *This* dilemma is to be faced by a large number of Christians in the not too distant future.

REVIEW

1 What question in the mind of Nebuchadnezzar was answered by his dream of an image of a man made of four metals?

2 What four nations that founded wide-spreading empires were represented by the four metals?

3 What nations were represented by the feet and toes made of mingled metal and clay?

4 How would you answer the objection that anyone could have made these predictions because history repeats itself?

5 May we expect the successful establishment of any united world government before the kingdom of God arrives?

6 How did God confirm the truthfulness of his dream to ambitious Nebuchadnezzar?

DANIEL 2

The prophecy of Nebuchadnezzar's metal man

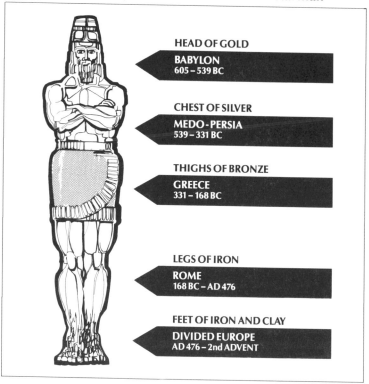

HEAD OF GOLD
BABYLON
605 – 539 BC

CHEST OF SILVER
MEDO - PERSIA
539 – 331 BC

THIGHS OF BRONZE
GREECE
331 – 168 BC

LEGS OF IRON
ROME
168 BC – AD 476

FEET OF IRON AND CLAY
DIVIDED EUROPE
AD 476 – 2nd ADVENT

3 God's people under pressure

THE FOUR KINGDOMS

Daniel 7:1 'Daniel had a dream.'

Daniel's dream covers the same outline as the king's dream. To represent the four successive kingdoms, four animals replace the four metals. But there is an important difference between the two dreams. The king was given a political outline. This would naturally concern him. The prophet, who knew by experience the difficulty of living as a worshipper of the God of heaven under the control of human governments, was given an outline of the experience of the people of God when living as servants of God in a world controlled by power politics.

4 '"The first was like a lion, and had eagle's wings. I watched till its wings were plucked off . . . and a man's heart was given to it."'

A winged lion was a popular symbol in Babylon at that time, and may still be seen displayed in museums. With the boldness of lions and the swiftness of eagles, Nabopolassar and his son Nebuchadnezzar had extended their control from the Persian Gulf to Syria and Egypt. But their successors were weak kings who settled down to enjoy the

DANIEL 7

7 In the first year of Belshazzar king of Babylon, Daniel had a dream and visions of his head *while* on his bed. Then he wrote down the dream, telling the main facts.

2 Daniel spoke, saying, 'I saw in my vision by night, and behold, the four winds of heaven were stirring up the Great Sea.

3 'And four great beasts came up from the sea, each different from the other.

4 'The first *was* like a lion, and had eagle's wings. I watched till its wings were plucked off; and it was lifted up from the earth and made to stand on two feet like a man, and a man's heart was given to it.

5 'And suddenly another beast, a second, like a bear. It was raised up on one side, and *had* three ribs in its mouth between its teeth. And they said thus to it: "Arise, devour much flesh!"

6 'After this I looked, and there was another, like a leopard, which had on its back four wings of a bird. The beast also had four heads, and dominion was given to it.

7 'After this I saw in the night visions, and behold, a fourth beast, dreadful and terrible, exceedingly strong. It had huge iron teeth; it was devouring, breaking in pieces, and trampling the residue with its feet. It *was* different from all the beasts that *were* before it, and it had ten horns.

8 'I was considering the horns, and there was another horn, a little one, coming up among them, before whom three of the first horns were plucked out by the roots. And there, in this horn, *were* eyes like the eyes of a man, and a mouth speaking pompous words.

9 'I watched till thrones were put in place,

wealth and luxury they had inherited.

5 "'A second, like a bear. It was raised up on one side, and had three ribs in its mouth between its teeth. And they said . . . 'Devour much flesh.''''

The lop-sided kingdom of Medo-Persia became the largest empire that had so far existed in the Middle East, by devouring the kingdom of Lydia in Asia Minor in 546, Babylon itself and its territories in Syria and Palestine in 538, and the ancient kingdom of Egypt in 525.

6 "'There was another, like a leopard, which had on its back four wings of a bird. The beast also had four heads, and dominion was given to it.''

The leopard is a fast-moving animal. To be given four wings in addition suggests the speed with which the young Alexander and his 35,000 soldiers conquered the whole Persian Empire. After Alexander died in 323 his generals tried to hold the empire together in the name of his young son. But eventually four generals established independent Greek governments. Cassander had Macedon and Greece, Lysymachus got Thrace, Bythinia and western Asia Minor, Ptolemy held Egypt and Palestine, and Seleucus at first held Persia but eventually established his capital in Antioch and

And the Ancient of Days was seated;
His garment *was* white as snow,
And the hair of his head *was* like pure wool.
His throne *was* a fiery flame,
Its wheels a burning fire;
10 A fiery stream issued
And came forth from before him.
A thousand thousands ministered to him;
Ten thousand times ten thousand stood before him.
The court was seated,
And the books were opened.
11 'I watched then because of the sound of the pompous words which the horn was speaking; I watched till the beast was slain, and its body destroyed and given to the burning flame.
12 'As for the rest of the beasts, they had their dominion taken away, yet their lives were prolonged for a season and a time.
13 'I was watching in the night visions,
And behold, *one* like the Son of Man,
Coming with the clouds of heaven!
He came to the Ancient of Days,
And they brought him near before him.
14 Then to him was given dominion
and glory and a kingdom,
That all peoples, nations, and languages should serve him.
His dominion *is* an everlasting dominion;
Which shall not pass away,
And his kingdom *the one*
Which shall not be destroyed.
15 'I, Daniel, was grieved in my spirit within *my* body, and the visions of my head troubled me.
16 'I came near to one of those who stood by, and asked him the truth of all this. So he told me and made known to me the interpretation of these things;
17 "Those great beasts, which are four, *are* four kings *which* arise out of the earth.
18 "But the saints of the Most High shall receive the kingdom, and possess the kingdom for ever, even for ever and ever."
19 'Then I wished to know the truth about the fourth beast, which was dif-

maintained a strong government in Syria and Mesopotamia, and in eastern Asia Minor.

7 *''A fourth beast . . . exceedingly strong . . . different from all the beasts before it.''*

The Roman Empire was not only more powerful than those before it. It was also different. They were all monarchies. It was, at first, a republic. Rome's first significant interference in the Hellenistic world was in 197 BC when she proclaimed the states of Greece free from the control of Macedon. In 190 she took away from Syria its territories in Asia Minor. In 168 she prevented Syria from invading Egypt simply by warning it, and in the same year she defeated Macedon and removed her king. In 133 the king of Pergamum, the last remaining significant power in Asia Minor, bequeathed his kingdom to the Romans when he died. In 65 BC Syria, and two years later, Judea, became provinces of the Roman Empire. Finally, the last of the great Hellenistic kingdoms, Egypt, became a Roman province in 30 BC. However, these eastern parts never received the distinctive marks of the Latin culture of Rome. This was foreseen by the prophecy as noted in verse 12:

12 *''As for the rest of the beasts, they had their dominion taken away, yet*

ferent from all the others, exceedingly dreadful, *with* its teeth of iron and its nails of bronze, *which* devoured, broke in pieces, and trampled the residue with its feet;

20 'and about the ten horns that *were* on its head, and *about* the other *horn* which came up, before which three fell, namely, that horn which had eyes and a mouth which spoke pompous words, whose appearance *was* greater than his fellows.

21 'I was watching; and the same horn was making war against the saints, and prevailing against them,

22 'until the Ancient of Days came, and a judgment was made *in favour* of the saints of the Most High, and the time came for the saints to possess the kingdom.

23 'Thus he said:
''The fourth beast shall be
A fourth kingdom on earth,
Which shall be different from all *other* kingdoms,
And shall devour the whole earth,
Trample it and break it in pieces.

24 The ten horns *are* ten kings
Who shall arise from this kingdom.
And another shall rise after them;
He shall be different from the first *ones*,
And shall subdue three kings.

25 He shall speak *pompous* words against the Most High,
Shall persecute the saints of the Most High,
And shall intend to change times and law.
Then the saints shall be given into his hand
For a time and times and half a time.

26 ''But the court shall be seated,
And they shall take away his dominion,
To consume and destroy *it* for ever.

27 ''Then the kingdom and dominion,
And the greatness of the kingdoms under the whole heaven,
Shall be given to the people,
the saints of the Most High.
His kingdom *is* an everlasting kingdom,
And all dominions shall serve and obey him.''

their lives were prolonged for a season and a time.'''

Babylon continued to exist till the seventh century AD. After that the beautiful city in which Daniel had lived became a

28 'This *is* the end of the account. As for me, Daniel, my thoughts greatly troubled me, and my countenance changed; but I kept the matter in my heart.'

desolate ruin and continues so to this day, as predicted in Jeremiah 50:1, 39, 40; 51:35-37. The Euphrates no longer flows through it, and its ruins in Iraq are now of interest only to archaeologists.

Persia received a great deal of attention from Roman soldiers, and many of them adopted her worship of the sun. Persia eventually became free again, and she exists today as modern Iran.

Greek continued to be spoken in Egypt and Syria for a long time, but Greece itself, though like Persia it still exists as an independent state, has never again become a dominant power. We must now return to what Daniel had to say about the fourth beast.

7 *'"It had ten horns."'*

These are mentioned again in verse 20, and in verse 24 interpreted as 'ten kings'. These represent the European nations which have developed from the distinctly Latin part of the empire. For centuries now the territory west of the Danube and the Rhine that was once western Rome has been occupied by separate national entities that have always averaged about ten in number. The original ten who took over when the imperial throne was vacated in AD 476 may be thought of as the Alemanni who settled in Alsace in 351, the Vandals who crossed over Europe and down through Spain to settle in north Africa by 429, the Burgundians who settled in western Switzerland and the Rhone valley after 443, the Anglo-Saxons who were settled in Britain by 449, the Franks who had reached the Seine by 455, the Lombards who occupied north Italy by 468, the Ostrogoths who entered the empire in 458 but took over southern Italy in 493, replacing the Heruli who had been there since 475. Seven of these still survive in Germany, France, Britain, Portugal, Spain, Switzerland and Italy. And today Holland, Belgium and Luxembourg may be thought of as making up the ten, and so included in the purview of prophecy for Revelation 12:3; 13:1 and 17:3, 12 continue to treat the horns not as seven, but as ten.

THE PAPACY

"Another horn, a little one."'

This is the great point of interest in Daniel's dream. The first three animals are described in four verses. The fourth and its horns, including the little horn, take nine verses, and of these five delineate the characteristics and activities of the little horn alone. The horns including the little horn are considered as an entity with the fourth beast. And as the European nations are continuations of the great Latin civilization, and the little horn appears as the pre-eminent perpetuator of the power and prestige of the Roman Empire, it must be the Roman Church.

"Coming up among them, before whom three of the first horns were plucked out."'

Christianity was born in the Middle East. Strong churches grew up in the old Greek-speaking parts such as Alexandria, Jerusalem, Caesarea, Antioch and Constantinople. But the Church of Rome arose to power among the ten tribes who took over the Latin west. Three of these, the Vandals, the Heruli and the Ostrogoths, were early converted by the missionary bishop, Ulfilas. But his Arian doctrine of the nature of Christ was not acceptable to Rome. When the Heruli tried to control the election of the bishop of Rome, he appealed to the emperor Zeno in Constantinople. Zeno suggested to the Ostrogoths that they deal with the Heruli. They displaced them in 493, but as Theodoric, the leader of the Ostrogoths, also insisted on having a controlling word about who should become bishop of Rome, another appeal went to Constantinople, to emperor Justinian. They were forced to leave Rome in 538 and, later, they were completely destroyed. In the meantime the same general, Belsarius, who was sent to deal with the Ostrogoths, had also destroyed the Vandals in 534. Thus three horns disappeared.

8 *"In this horn, were eyes like the eyes of a man, and a mouth speaking pompous words."'*

In 'the eyes and mouth' we may recognize the political

foresight, shrewd diplomacy and presumptuous claims that have long marked papal history. Imperial Rome had been the centre of the civilized world for centuries. When Romulus Augustulus abdicated a year after the arrival of the Heruli, the bishop of Rome became, in effect, the unofficial successor of Caesar. The Emperor of Constantinople, Justinian, not only answered the bishop's request to relieve him of the Vandals and the Ostrogoths, but passing over the bishops of the eastern parts, he recognized the bishop of Rome as the chief bishop of the Christian Church. This was in 533.

20   *'"(His) appearance was greater than his fellows."'*

After the Franks became Christian, the Pope crowned Charlemagne as Emperor of the Romans in AD 800. In this way the Pope formed, under his own control, a Holy Roman Empire in which for a thousand years the rulers of Europe in theory governed by permission of the Pope of Rome. This ambitious plan reached its zenith under Pope Gregory VII (1073-85), who first enforced the theory that the Pope could depose kings. And not long after that, Pope Innocent III (1198-1216) forced King John of England to submit to him and, in return, released him from the Magna Carta wrung from him by his barons. And in 1570 Pope Pius V actually attempted to depose Queen Elizabeth I and forbade her subjects to obey her.

25   *'"He . . . shall persecute the saints of the Most High."'*
21   *'"The same horn was making war against the saints, and prevailing against them."'*

The doctrine of the Catholic Church, as formulated by the great theologian Thomas Aquinas, is that all baptized Christians, whether professed Catholics or not, are subjects of the Mother Church, and she has the full right to punish them, even to the death penalty.

Many Huguenots in France in the seventeenth century were dealt with on this basis. The historian Lecky, recalling the 31,000 burned at the instigation of the Spanish Inquisition, the 50,000 who died in the Netherlands when Charles V, then the Holy Roman Emperor, attempted to stamp out the Protestant heresy, the papal instigation of the massacre of a million Waldenses, and the papal celebration of the massacre of

80,000 Huguenots on the eve of St Bartholomew, declared that the Church of Rome had shed more innocent blood than any other institution that had ever existed among mankind.

Note this from *The Catholic Encyclopedia*, vol. XIV, page 763: 'If in medieval times the Church adopted sterner measures against formal heretics, apostates, and schismatics, than she adopts today, she did this not as a private individual, but as the legitimate governing authority, within whose sphere also fell the administration of penal justice.'

25   ' " 'He . . . shall intend to change times and law.' " '

Keenan's *Catechism*, published by Burns and Oates in 1914, actually boasts that the Catholic Church has the power to make such changes else 'she could not have substituted the observance of Sunday, the first day of the week, for the observance of Saturday, the seventh day — a change for which there is no Scriptural authority.' (Page 125.)

It is a fact of history that the observance of Sunday in place of the Sabbath began in Rome about a century after the resurrection of Jesus. The custom gradually spread from Rome until most Christians everywhere gathered for worship and celebrated the Lord's Supper on both the Bible Sabbath and the new 'Lord's Day' every week. In Rome, however, Sunday came to be preferred above the Sabbath, and by the fourth century the Sabbath ceased to be observed in Rome and in Alexandria. Everywhere else both days continued to be observed until about 600. Rome, however, repeatedly urged her custom of observing only Sunday, thus setting aside a plain requirement of the Law of God. Nevertheless, both days continued to be observed in certain places in England and Ireland until AD 600, in the East and in Scotland until 1100, and in Ethiopia until 1700.

' " 'The saints shall be given into his hand for a time and times and half a time.' " '

This period is mentioned again in Revelation 12:6 and 14 as three and a half years and as twelve hundred and sixty days. Compare the various modern versions. In the symbolic language of these prophecies, in the same way as beasts and horns represent nations, a prophetic day stands for a calendar year. Daniel's contemporary prophet, Ezekiel, was specifically given this measurement. (Ezek. 4:5, 6.) In this way the reader is warned that this oppression might last for a period of twelve and a half centuries. This is the awful possibility that Jesus referred to in Matthew 24:21, 22. Only after the Ostrogoths were driven out of Rome was the bishop of Rome able to exercise some degree of authority. After that, step by step, he achieved more and more control over international affairs in Europe. Eventually he was insisting that not only bishops but also princes and kings should carry out his wishes. He pronounced death sentences on those whose consciences made them differ from church customs. But all this exercise of authority was greatly reduced, exactly 1,260 years after AD 538, when General Berthier, on behalf of revolutionary France, took the Pope prisoner in the year 1798. The papal supremacy had lasted just 'three and a half times'.

THE PRE-ADVENT JUDGEMENT

9-10 *"'I watched till thrones were put in place, and the Ancient of Days was seated . . . the court was seated, and the books were opened.'"*

All the history of man's attempt to rule must collapse when confronted with the throne of God. There can be only one Judge, the eternally self-existent One. When in His awful majesty He sits surrounded by myriads of angel witnesses with their unerring testimony, then the pompous words of men will count for nothing.

Though divine judgement will have its final session after the second resurrection at the end of the millennium (Rev. 20:5, 12) its opening session must take place *before* the second coming of Jesus, for those who are to be raised in the first resurrection will be 'the blessed and the holy' who have died believing in Jesus. (Rev. 20:6; 1 Thess. 4:15-17.) The apostle John will tell us that while the Gospel of salvation is still being preached a message is due to be given to the world that the hour of judgement has actually arrived. (Rev. 14:6, 7.) And in his very next visions Daniel will be given the specific date at which this pre-advent judgement is to begin, namely AD 1844. At that time Jesus began the final work of His priestly ministry before the throne which will end in His receiving the kingdom of the saints.

11 '"I watched then because of the sound of the pompous words which the horn was speaking."'

The prophet's attention seems to have been distracted from the judgement scene by specific blasphemies spoken after the judgement had actually begun. Could it be that he heard the claim of Pope Leo XIII in 1894 that he held on earth the place of Almighty God? Or was it the declaration of the Vatican Council in 1870 that the Pope is infallible when he pronounces authoritatively on matters of doctrine or morals?

'"I watched till the beast was slain, and its body destroyed and given to the burning flame."'

This verse makes it clear that though the earlier empires, having lost their dominion, might yet continue to exist for a season, the fourth, Rome, in its ecclesiastical phase, will continue to be active until it comes to a sudden and complete end when Jesus returns in glory. (2 Thess. 1:7, 8.)

13, 14 '"One like the Son of Man, coming with the clouds of heaven . . . came to the Ancient of Days, and they brought him near before him. Then to him was given dominion and glory and a kingdom . . . and his dominion is an everlasting dominion."'

Jesus' favourite title for Himself was 'the Son of Man'. He used it some eighty times in the gospels. It emphasizes His permanent union with humanity. He is our Advocate in heaven. (1 John 2:1.) He is the nobleman who has gone to a far country to receive a kingdom. (Luke 19:12.) When He returns to earth it will be as 'the Root and Offspring of David', the Messianic King so long awaited by His people. (Rev. 22:16.) This is the satisfying climax of the vision. Read its final words and rejoice.

22 '"The Ancient of Days came, and judgement was made in favour of the saints of the Most High, and the time came for the saints to possess the kingdom."'
27 '"And the greatness of the kingdoms under the whole heaven, shall be given to the people, the saints of the Most High.'"'

Jesus said: '"Do not fear, little flock, for it is your Father's good pleasure to give you the kingdom."' (Luke 12:32.) And to this the apostle added: 'If we endure, we shall also reign with him.' (2 Tim. 2:12.) He wants us to be 'with Him' then. It all depends on whether we decide to be 'with Him' here.

In this chapter the sufferings of God's people are shown to end in their complete vindication, and the enjoyment of the eternal reward. In the visions of John a period of acute persecution just before the return of Jesus is described, but it ends, as in Daniel, with a glorious picture of divine blessing and a reign of peace.

REVIEW

1   Can you name three kingdoms conquered by Medo-Persia?

2   What four geographic areas were ruled by Greek rulers who took over after the death of Alexander?

3   What nations now occupy the western part of what was once the Roman Empire?

4   In what ways may the papal horn be considered as a continuation of the Roman Empire?

5   How does the Catholic Church justify her attempt in the past to dominate and punish Christians who disagreed with her teachings?

6   Can you name the steps by which Sabbath observance was gradually displaced by Sunday observance?

7   What specific events marked the beginning and the end of the period of papal power?

8   What will be the verdict of the pre-advent judgement concerning the people of God?

4 The sanctuary ministry subverted

Daniel 8:1 *'A vision appeared to me . . . Daniel . . . after the one that appeared to me the first time.'*
16, 17 *'''Gabriel . . . said to me, Understand, son of man, that the vision refers to the time of the end.''' '*

Daniel's previous vision, which had pictured the people of God under heavy-handed rulers, had left him troubled. (Dan. 7:28.) Two years later, further light was given him. And lest he, or we, should be inclined to think that the main burden of the vision was for those early times, Gabriel cautions him, and us, to expect its main application to come at the end of time. And the angel of prophecy hastens to interpret the early part and move on.

A REVIEW

3 *'I lifted up my eyes and saw . . . a ram with two horns . . . but one was higher than the other, and the higher one came up last.'*
20 *'''The ram which you saw, having the two horns — they are the kings of Media and Persia.''' '*

This vision was given during the reign of the last king of Babylon, so it begins with the Medo-Persians. This incidentally confirms our interpretations of the previous dreams of the king and the prophet. As to the kings of

DANIEL 8 and 9

8 In the third year of the reign of King Belshazzar a vision appeared *to* me — to me, Daniel — after the one that appeared to me the first time.

2 I saw in the vision, and it so happened while I was looking, that I *was* in Shushan, the citadel, which *is* in the province of Elam; and I saw in the vision that I was by the River Ulai.

3 Then I lifted my eyes and saw, and there, standing beside the river, was a ram which had two horns, and the two horns *were* high; but one *was* higher than the other, and the higher *one* came up last.

4 I saw the ram pushing westward, northward, and southward, so that no beast could withstand him; nor *was* there *any* that could deliver from his hand, but he did according to his will and became great.

5 And as I was considering, suddenly a male goat came from the west, across the surface of the whole earth, without touching the ground; and the goat *had* a remarkable horn between his eyes.

6 Then he came to the ram that had two horns, which I had seen standing beside the river, and ran at him with furious power.

7 And I saw him confronting the ram; he was moved with rage against him, attacked the ram, and broke his two horns. There was no power in the ram to withstand him, but he cast him down to the ground and trampled him; and there was no one that could deliver the ram from his hand.

8 Therefore the male goat grew very great; but when he became strong, the large horn was broken, and in place of it four notable ones came up towards the four winds of heaven.

33

Media and Persia, up until the time of the vision the Medians had been in the ascendancy. Kyaxares I and Astyages had reigned. It was Kyaxares II, known to us as Darius the Median, who would take over the kingdom from Belshazzar several years later. (Dan. 5:30, 31.) Thereafter the next rulers would be the Persians, Cyrus, Cambyses, Gomates, Darius Hystaspis, Xerxes and Artaxerxes. As the angel said, the higher horn came up last. Iran is modern Persia. The Kurds are probably descended from the Medes.

4 'I saw the ram pushing westward, northward, and southward, so that no beast could withstand him.'

Kyaxares had already extended Median power westward by dividing Assyria with Nabopollassar in 612 BC. He pushed further westward to the boundary of Lydia in Asia Minor by 585. Then, under Astyages, Cyrus led the armies of Medo-Persia right through Lydia to the Aegean Sea in 547. Northward, Kyaxares and Astyages had pushed into Armenia and Cappadocia, and Darius Hystaspis would actually push right through Thrace up to the Danube by 508. Southward it was Cyrus who conquered Babylon in 538 and Cambyses who moved through Egypt as far as Ethiopia by 525. So by the

9 And out of one of them came a little horn which grew exceedingly great towards the south, towards the east, and towards the Glorious *Land*.

10 And it grew up to the host of heaven; and it cast down *some* of the host and *some* of the stars to the ground, and trampled them.

11 He even exalted *himself* as high as the Prince of the host; and by him the daily *sacrifices* were taken away, and the place of his sanctuary was cast down.

12 Because of transgression, an army was given over *to the horn* to oppose the daily *sacrifices;* and he cast truth down to the ground. He did *all this* and prospered.

13 Then I heard a holy one speaking; and *another* holy one said to that certain *one* who was speaking, 'How long *will* the vision be, *concerning* the daily *sacrifices* and the transgression of desolation, the giving of both the sanctuary and the host to be trampled underfoot?'

14 And he said to me, 'For two thousand three hundred days; then the sanctuary shall be cleansed.'

15 Now it happened, when I, Daniel, had seen the vision and was seeking the meaning, that suddenly there stood before me one having the appearance of a man.

16 And I heard a man's voice between *the banks of* the Ulai, who called, and said, 'Gabriel, make this *man* understand the vision.'

17 So he came near where I stood, and when he came I was afraid and fell on my face; but he said to me, 'Understand, son of man, that the vision *refers* to the time of the end.'

18 Now, as he was speaking with me, I was in a deep sleep with my face to the ground; but he touched me, and stood me upright.

19 And he said, 'Look, I am making known to you what shall happen in the latter time of the indignation; for at the appointed time the end *shall be*

20 'The ram which you saw, having the

time of Xerxes the empire extended from Ethiopia to India. (Esther 1:1.)

5, 6 'Suddenly a male goat came from the west, across the surface of the whole earth. . . . He came to the ram . . . and ran at him with furious power.'
21 '"The male goat is the kingdom of Greece. The large horn that is between its eyes is the first king."'

It was Alexander the Great who raised Greece to world power. In attacking the Medo-Persian Empire he completely subdued all the territory, mopping up as he went along. He first subdued all of Asia Minor, then cleared the coast of the western mediterranean by going down through Syria, Phoenicia and Palestine. On the way he took time to destroy all that remained of the city of Tyre in order to build a causeway to reach the island city and break its power. He also reduced Gaza and obtained the submission of Jerusalem. He was so pleased when the high priest showed him Daniel's prediction of his success that he made the Jews first-class citizens of the new city Alexandria that he built in Egypt after he had subdued it. After that he dealt with Mesopotamia, Babylonia, Persia, Media, Parthia and Bactria.

8 'The male goat grew very great; but when he became strong, the large horn was broken, and in place of it four notable ones came up.'

two horns — *they are* the kings of Media and Persia.
21 'And the male goat *is* the kingdom of Greece. The large horn that *is* between its eyes *is* the first king.
22 'As for the broken *horn* and the four that stood up in its place, four kingdoms shall arise out of that nation, but not with its power.
23 'And in the latter time of their kingdom,
When the transgressors have reached their fullness,
A king shall arise,
Having fierce features,
Who understands sinister schemes.
24 'His power shall be mighty,
 but not by his own power;
He shall destroy fearfully,
And shall prosper and thrive;
He shall destroy the mighty,
 and *also* the holy people.
25 'Through his cunning
He shall cause deceit to prosper under his hand;
And he shall magnify *himself* in his heart.
He shall destroy many in *their* prosperity.
He shall even rise against the Prince of princes;
But he shall be broken without *human* hand.
26 'And the vision of the evenings and mornings
Which was told is true;
Therefore seal up the vision,
For it *refers* to many days *in the future.*'
27 And I, Daniel, fainted and was sick for days; afterwards I arose and went about the king's business. I was astonished by the vision, but no one understood it.

9 In the first year of Darius the son of Ahasuerus, of the lineage of the Medes, who was made king over the realm of the Chaldeans —
2 in the first year of his reign I, Daniel, understood by the books the number of

22 "'As for the broken horn and the four that stood up in its place, four kingdoms shall arise out of the nation, but not with its power.'"

We have already become familiar with the four 'notable' kingdoms in Syria, Egypt, Asia Minor and Macedonia. Other smaller, less 'notable' areas that became independent include Rhodes and Pontus, Epirus, Achaia, Aetolia and Athens. Thus the Greek-speaking kingdom lacked any centralized authority, and eventually all its parts were gobbled up by the next claimant to universal control.

23 "'In the latter time of their kingdom, when the transgressors have reached their fullness, a king shall arise, having fierce features, who understands sinister schemes.'"

The Hellenistic world had its day of opportunity. Though Jewish officials rose high in the service of the Greek kings of Egypt and Syria, we do not know of anyone like Daniel or Esther who had a saving influence on them. Instead the Syrian kings tried to force Hellenization (Greek language and culture) on the Jews, the kings of Egypt became notorious for their degeneracy, and the Greeks became morally debased. As with the Amorites, the Assyrians, and the Babylonians, the figures in God's account of their iniquity reached a certain level, and their accounts

the years *specified* by the word of the Lord, *given* through Jeremiah the prophet, that he would accomplish seventy years in the desolations of Jerusalem.

3 Then I set my face towards the Lord God to make request by prayer and supplications, with fasting, sackcloth, and ashes.

4 And I prayed to the Lord my God, and made confession, and said, 'O Lord, great and awesome God, who keeps his covenant and mercy with those who love him, and with those who keep his commandments,

5 'we have sinned and committed iniquity, we have done wickedly and rebelled, even by departing from your precepts and your judgements.

13 'As *it is* written in the Law of Moses, all this disaster has come upon us; yet we have not made our prayer before the Lord our God, that we might turn from our iniquities and understand your truth.

14 'Therefore the Lord has kept the disaster in mind, and brought it upon us; for the Lord our God *is* righteous in all the works which he does, though we have not obeyed his voice.

16 'O Lord, according to all your righteousness, I pray, let your anger and your fury be turned away from your city Jerusalem, your holy mountain; because for our sins, and for the iniquities of our fathers, Jerusalem and your people *have become* a reproach to all *who are* around us.

17 'Now therefore, our God, hear the prayer of your servant, and his supplications, and for the Lord's sake cause your face to shine on your sanctuary, which is desolate.

18 'O my God, incline your ear and hear; open your eyes and see our desolations, and the city which is called by your name; for we do not present our supplications before you because of our righteous deeds, but because of your great mercies.

19 'O Lord, hear! O Lord, forgive! O

were closed. (Gen. 15:16; Jonah 1:2; 3:4; Nahum 1:1, 2, 9; Jer. 15:17, 18; Dan. 5:27, 28.)

ROME, PAGAN AND PAPAL

9 *'And out of one of them came a little horn which grew exceedingly great towards the south . . . the east . . . and towards the Glorious land.'*

This little horn must represent Rome in both its pagan and its papal phases. The story begins with Imperial Rome's expansion towards Egypt in the south, Syria and Mesopotamia in the east, and even towards the Glorious land, Judea.

Lord, listen and act! Do not delay for your own sake, my God, for your city and your people are called by your name.'

20 Now while I *was* speaking, praying, and confessing my sin and the sin of my people Israel, and presenting my supplication before the Lord my God for the holy mountain of my God,

21 yes, while I *was* speaking in prayer, the man Gabriel, whom I had seen in the vision at the beginning, being caused to fly swiftly, reached me about the time of the evening offering.

10 *'It cast down some of the host and of the stars to the ground, and trampled on them.'*
24 *'"He shall destroy fearfully . . . he shall destroy the mighty, and also the holy people."'*

Imperial Rome destroyed a million Jews in the first century and three million Christians in the next two centuries. Ecclesiastical Rome in the Middle Ages destroyed untold millions of so-called heretics.

11 *'He even exalted himself as high as the Prince of the host.'*
25 *'"He shall even rise against the Prince of princes."'*

This must refer to 'the prince' called Messiah in Daniel 9:25 and Michael in Daniel 12:1. It was the Roman governor, Pilate, who was legally responsible for the crucifixion of 'the king of the Jews'. It is the Bishop of Rome who has openly assumed the offices of Christ as the mediator between God and man. The whole Catholic doctrine of priestly orders is wrong. In the New Testament Church no apostle, elder, deacon or other church officer was ever called a 'priest'. This title was reserved almost exclusively for Christ Himself. (Heb. 2:17; 3:1; 4:14-16; 5:5-10; 7:11; 8:1-6; 9:11, 12; 10:11, 12, 19, 23.) Our Great High Priest does not need earthly priests to take His place, for He exercises a 'perpetual priesthood', being 'always alive to make intercession'. (Heb. 7:24, 25.) In a lesser sense and only a few times, the word 'priest' is used for all true believers, but not for any officer of the church. (1 Peter 1:1, 2 and 2:5, 7-10.)

'And by him the daily sacrifices were taken away.'

'By him' is rendered as 'from him' in the RSV, NIV as in the AV margin. Moffat says the little horn 'deprived' the Prince of the daily sacrifice. Actually the word 'sacrifice' has been added to the text by the translators. Daniel has only the word *tamid*, which is rendered as 'daily' in the AV, RAV, Moff, NIV, as 'continual' in the RSV, 'regular' in the REB, and 'perpetual' in the JB. It refers to very much more than the daily sacrifices offered on the altar.

Besides the sacrifices there were many other parts of the sanctuary services which are qualified by the word *tamid* in the Old Testament records. The priestly ministry of Christ was indeed prefigured by the 'regular burnt-offering', (Num. 28:2, 3) offered 'day by day continually'. (Exod. 29:38.) This reminded the people of their constant dependence on the blood of the Lamb. The shew bread, which was to be on the table 'always', (Exod. 25:30) symbolized the believer's daily sustenance, the Bread of Life. (John 6:35, 57.) Morning and evening the 'perpetual incense' made the place of worship fragrant at the hour of prayer, (Exod. 30:7, 8; Luke 1:9, 10). And in the heavenly temple it is only Christ's perfect righteousness that can make our prayers acceptable. (Rev. 8:3, 4.) The seven-branched lampstand was the source of light in the sanctuary both day and night. It was to burn 'continually'. (Exod. 27:20; Lev. 24:2.) Jesus said, '''I am the light of the world.''' (John 8:12; 9:5.) It is in the presence of the living Saviour that we may walk safely. And, perhaps most precious of all, the twelve precious stones on the ornament that Aaron wore over his heart, pointed to the way in which our Saviour carries upon his heart the name of every one of His people. (Exod. 28:15-21, 29, 30; Heb. 4:14-16; 7:25; 9:24.) Our gracious Lord would have each of His children look to Him personally, but this *tamid* has been taken away from Him by a system of worship that teaches the faithful to look to magical sacraments, good works such as prayer, fasting, and almsgiving, confession to a priest, the miraculous sacrifice of the Mass, and the motherly mediation of Mary.

'And the place of his sanctuary was cast down.'

The sanctuary built by Moses, and the temple built by Solomon, were divinely-ordained representations of the temple in heaven where Christ would minister after His ascension. (Heb. 8:1-5.) Until our Lord took human flesh and became both our Sacrifice and our Priest, the earthly sanctuary and its priestly ministries taught men about the saving work of Christ. When Jesus offered His own sacrifice forever, the veil of the temple was supernaturally torn to indicate that Israel's system of worship had reached its climax and would be superceded by the true tabernacle in heaven where Christ would fulfil all that the earthly service has symbolized. (Matt. 27:51; Heb. 9:24-26; 10:11, 12.) Making people think that the priest actually repeats the sacrifice of Christ in the Mass, and that confession may be made to the priest and forgiveness received from him, only takes away from our Lord Jesus Christ the loving personal ministry He waits to give to every believing soul.

12 *'And he cast down truth to the ground.'*

In Jesus' great prayer, often called His high priestly prayer, He said, '"Your word is truth."' (John 17:17.) The history of how the written truth of Scripture has been cast down by the Church is a sad one. From the twelfth century onwards various popes prohibited the use of the Bible in the vernacular because such use by the Waldensians and later by Protestants, revealed the erroneous doctrines taught by the Church. People began to question the adoration of images, natural immortality, eternal torment, purgatory, auricular confession, the sacrifice of the Mass, and Sunday sacredness. To try to limit the damage, the Council of Trent decreed in 1546 that none were to interpret Scripture contrary to the teaching of the Church. The Encyclical of Pius XI in 1943 appears to reverse this trend, but it must be noted that in urging priests to study and preach from Scripture and encouraging the laity to read the Bible, he made it plain that the interpretation of Scripture must be on the basis of nearly two thousand years of Catholic exegesis. Happily, this new freedom has in many instances had excellent results, as the true teachings of God's Word have again become apparent.

GOD'S DAY OF FINAL RECKONING

When David was overwhelmed with trouble and found comfort by resting by faith in God, he cried out: 'Your way, O God, is in the sanctuary.' (Ps. 77:13.) Fifty chapters in Moses' writings describe the details of the divinely-ordained plan of the sanctuary and its worship. In the New Testament, the whole book of Hebrews is devoted to the ministry of that 'better' priest, who after He had offered a 'better' sacrifice, went on to become for us a 'new and living way' into the presence of God. It is against this Priest, chosen by God, that papal teachings and practices have had their most disastrous effect. The query is now raised in the prophet's hearing: What is to be done about this? The prophet heard the answer given, and we must hear it too.

13 'I heard a holy one speaking; and another holy one said to that certain one who was speaking, "How long will the vision be, concerning the daily sacrifices and the transgression of desolation, the giving of both the sanctuary and the host to be trodden underfoot?"'

The answer concerning the oppression of the host of God's people is answered in a similar exchange between two heavenly beings in Daniel 12:5-7. The answer is that the heavy hand of the little horn would be curbed in 1798. So we await only the answer concerning the sanctuary.

14 'And he said to me, "For two thousand three hundred days; then the sanctuary shall be cleansed."'

As this period, counted like the 1,260 days, a prophetic day representing a calendar year, would last for twenty-three centuries, we are alerted to the fact that the cleansing of the sanctuary deals with something much larger than anything Rome could have done to make it necessary. The period itself is almost twice as long as the papal supremacy.

OF WHAT IS THE SANCTUARY TO BE CLEANSED?

Daniel's unique use of the word *tamid* is of importance here. As we have already noted, it was all those elements of our High Priest's ministry that are qualified by the word 'daily' or 'continual' that the Church has taken away from Him by its doctrines and practices. But there is another very important activity that took place day after day at the sanctuary which is not once in Scripture qualified by the word *tamid*. It is the personal sin-offerings brought by individual Israelites described fully in Leviticus 4:27-31, and again in verses 32-35. In this simple service the conscience-smitten sinner brought an innocent substitute to die in his place. He laid his hands upon the head of this lamb or little goat, thereby appointing it his representative as a sinner, and then killed it himself. The priest sprinkled some of the blood on the altar, and later ate part of the flesh. (Lev. 6:25, 26.) In this way the responsibility for confessed sins was symbolically transferred to the altar, and even to the priest. (Num. 18:1, 9; Zech. 3:1-4.) When the priest himself needed to rid himself of sin, whether on an ordinary day or before ministering on the day of atonement, he used a bullock, and the blood was brought into the sanctuary itself. (Lev. 4:3-7; 16:11, 15.) The sin of individuals, thus personally acknowledged, were in this way transferred to the sanctuary, thereby defiling it. This accumulated record of 'uncleanness' because of 'all their sins' was cleansed away and finally removed from the sanctuary only on the annual day of atonement. (Lev. 16:30, 34.)

As we have already noted, this freeing of individuals from the responsibility for their personal sins, which we call forgiveness, is never qualified by *tamid*, though it went on day after day. It could, therefore, not be included in what the little horn took away from the sanctuary ministry of our Lord. God did not permit the precious privilege of personal access to the merits of the crucified Saviour to be taken away from His people. Thus, down through the years, members of the Church of Rome may have been robbed of the comfort of knowing Jesus as their caring Priest, (Heb. 2:18; 4:15, 16), but they have always been aware of His sacrifice made at the cross, and thus of the personal pardon possible. And as they have laid their sins on Jesus, the responsibility for them has been transferred to the heavenly sanctuary thereby defiling that holy place, and making it necessary that eventually it would have to be 'cleansed'.

The question may be asked, Could anything in heaven become defiled and need cleansing? The answer is plain: 'It was necessary that the copies of the things in the heavens should be purified with these (the "blood of calves and goats", verse 19), but the heavenly things themselves with better sacrifices than these. For Christ has not entered the holy places made with hands, which are copies of the true, but into heaven itself.' (Heb. 9:23, 24; Rev. 5:6.) Thus, in heaven's day of reckoning, described as a judgement in the vision of Daniel 7, the Son of Man would represent His people, obtain a judgement in their favour, and their sins would be blotted out. The Day of Atonement ceremony, in which the sanctuary is cleansed of all the sins of all the people, is another picture of the same blessed event. And when the record of the sins of God's people has been dealt with in the process of the judgement which completes the work of the sanctuary in heaven, we may say with the RSV that heaven has been 'restored to its rightful state' of purity, or we may say with the AV and RAV that the sanctuary has been 'cleansed'. The latter word fits the symbolism of Leviticus 16:30.

THE ENDING OF THE 2,300 DAYS

Gabriel plainly cautioned Daniel that the vision would reach to ' "the time of the end" ', (Dan. 8:17) and that the cleansing of the sanctuary would only take place ' "many days in the future" '. (Verse 26.) Daniel naturally thought this must be something to do with the only sanctuary he knew, the one destroyed by Nebuchadnezzar in 586 BC. Thus Daniel made the temple in Jerusalem the object of his study and his prayers.

Daniel 9:2-4, 17-19 'I, Daniel, understood by the books . . . that he would accomplish seventy years in the desolations of Jerusalem. Then I set my face towards the Lord God . . . and I prayed . . . "Now therefore, our God, hear the prayer of your servant . . . and cause your face to shine on your sanctuary, which is desolate . . . . Do not delay for your own sake . . . for your city and your people are called by your name." '

Clearly Daniel's concern was about Israel's people, their city and sanctuary, lest they should continue to be trodden down and desolate. It is in answering these concerns that Gabriel solves the problem about when the 2,300 days would begin and end, and incidentally to what sanctuary they refer.

We have already noted in chapter one that Gabriel first assured Daniel that Jerusalem would be rebuilt, and he foretold the decree of 457 BC. He also told him that in the 490 years beginning from that date, reconciliation for iniquity would be made and everlasting righteousness made possible, the messianic prophecies would be fulfilled and the true sanctuary service inaugurated. When Gabriel said, 'Seventy weeks are determined for your people' he used a word with reference to the 490 years that appears nowhere else in the Bible. In other literature of the period the word rendered 'determined' in the AV and RAV occurs with the meaning 'to cut' and 'to cut off'.

As Daniel's perplexity was with the long unexplained period leading up to the cleansing of the sanctuary it is logical to understand that Gabriel meant to tell Daniel that the 490 years of Jewish probation were cut off from the beginning of it. He had already made it clear that the period itself that would reach to the cleansing of the sanctuary would extend to 'the time of the end'. (Daniel 8:17; 8:26-9:3; 9:24.)

Everything fits together. Before the end of the 490 years, Messiah would come, and having offered Himself as 'a lamb without blemish and without spot', (1 Peter 1:19) He would anoint His own sanctuary and begin His daily ministry there. This would continue for the 1,800 years that are left of the 2,300 after subtracting the 490 cut off as a period of extra probation for the Jews till Messiah arrived. This would reach from AD 34 to AD 1844. Thenceforward He would serve in heaven as the High Priest of His people and provide daily assurance, continual sustenance, and perpetual acceptance. All this gracious ministry might be taken away from by the mistaken efforts of religious leaders, but the mistaken teachings of the Church would not prevent Him from remitting the sins of those who sought Him personally for pardon. And finally, when the 2,300 years expired in 1844, He would begin His final work of cleansing the heavenly sanctuary of the confessed sins of His believing people, claim judgement in their favour, and return to give them the kingdom to which every prophecy has pointed. In this final ministry He is still engaged. Soon the list of the names of the saved in the Lamb's Book of life will be complete, and His sanctuary ministry will be ended.

REVIEW

1 Did the geographical expansions of the Medo-Persian Empire match the predictions made in the prophecy?

2 How does God determine when a national power should be replaced by another?

3 What facts of history fulfilled the prediction that the pagan-papal horn would 'destroy fearfully'?

4 What other sanctuary services besides the animal sacrifices are described in Scripture as taking place 'daily' or 'continually'?

5 What Roman Catholic practices and teachings obscure the various elements of the continual ministry of our Lord in heaven?

6 Make a list of five or six other Catholic teachings in which Scripture truth has been cast to the ground.

7 How did the oft-repeated sin-offerings at the Jewish temple produce a record that needed cleansing away on the annual day of atonement?

8 When, according to the angel, would heaven's great day of atonement take place?

9 Do the verses in Daniel, to which Jesus drew attention, point accurately to the date of His atoning sacrifice, and also give us the date for His priestly ministry of reconciliation?

DANIEL 8:14

'Unto 2,300 days, then shall the sanctuary be cleansed'

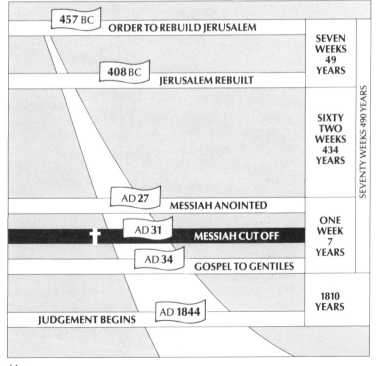

457 BC — ORDER TO REBUILD JERUSALEM

SEVEN WEEKS 49 YEARS

408 BC — JERUSALEM REBUILT

SIXTY TWO WEEKS 434 YEARS

AD 27 — MESSIAH ANOINTED

AD 31 — MESSIAH CUT OFF

ONE WEEK 7 YEARS

AD 34 — GOSPEL TO GENTILES

1810 YEARS

JUDGEMENT BEGINS — AD 1844

SEVENTY WEEKS 490 YEARS

5 The conquests of the kings

Daniel's last vision took place in the third year of Cyrus, king of Persia, according to Daniel 10:1. The angel told him then that the '"vision refers to many days yet to come."' (Dan. 10:14.) He began:

PERSIANS

Daniel 11:2 '"Now I will tell you the truth: Behold three more kings will arise in Persia."'

They were Cambyses, who conquered Egypt in 525, Gomates, a usurper who ruled for only eight months in 522, Darius Hystaspis, who thoroughly organized the empire and attempted to take over Greece but was defeated at the famous battle of Marathon.

'"The fourth . . . far richer than them all . . . shall stir up all against the realm of Greece."'

Xerxes the Great was indeed wealthy, and he mounted a tremendous assault, but his formidable forces were held up at Thermopylae by the Spartans and defeated in a sea battle by the Athenians. Persia did not invade Europe again, but the Greeks did not forget.

DANIEL 11 and 12

11 'Also in the first year of Darius the Mede, I, *even* I, stood up to confirm and strengthen him.)

2 'And now I will tell you the truth: Behold, three more kings will arise in Persia, and the fourth shall be far richer than *them* all; by his strength, through his riches, he shall stir up against the realm of Greece.

3 'Then a mighty king shall arise, who shall rule with great dominion, and do according to his will.

4 'And when he has arisen, his kingdom shall be broken up and divided towards the four winds of heaven, but not among his posterity nor according to his dominion with which he ruled; for his kingdom shall be uprooted, even for others besides these.

5 'Then the king of the South shall become strong, as well as *one* of his princes; and he shall gain power over him and have dominion. His dominion *shall be* a great dominion.

6 'And at the end of *some* years they shall join forces, for the daughter of the king of the South shall go to the king of the North to make an agreement; but she shall not retain the power of her authority, and neither he nor his authority shall stand; but she shall be given up, with those who brought her, and with him who begot her, and with him who strengthened her in *those* times.

7 'But from a branch of her roots *one* shall arise in his place, who shall come with an army, enter the fortress of the king of the North, and deal with them and prevail.

8 'And he shall also carry their gods captive to Egypt, with their princes and

GREEKS

3, 4 '"A mighty king shall arise, who shall rule with great dominion . . . . His kingdom shall be broken up and divided towards the four winds."'

This is Alexander and the four kingdoms established by his generals.

5 '"Then the king of the South shall become strong."'

15 '"The king of the North shall come . . . and the forces of the South shall not withstand him."'

The next verses 5 to 15 give many interesting details concerning the relationship between Egypt and Syria, the kingdoms immediately north and south of Judea. To go over them all would make this book too long. If the reader wishes to study them he could choose one of the larger books listed in the Bibliography.

ROMANS

16 '"He who comes against him . . . shall stand in the Glorious Land."'

The vision seems to refer to the coming of the Romans from here onwards — the Roman emperors and the Roman popes.

22 '"They shall be swept away before him . . . also the prince of the covenant."'

This must be a reference to the death of Christ under the authority of pagan Rome.

31 '"They shall defile the sanctuary . . . take away the daily sacrifices . . .

their precious articles of silver and gold; and he shall continue *more* years than the king of the North.

9 'Then the king of the North shall come to the kingdom of the king of the South, but shall return to his own land.

10 'However his sons shall stir up strife, and assemble a multitude of great forces; and *one* shall certainly come and overwhelm and pass through; then he shall return to his fortress and stir up strife.

11 'And the king of the South shall be moved with rage, and go out and fight with him, with the king of the North, who shall muster a great multitude; but the multitude shall be given into the hand of his *enemy*.

12 'When he has taken away the multitude, his heart will be lifted up; and he will cast down tens of thousands, but he will not prevail.

13 'For the king of the North will return and muster a multitude greater than the former, and shall certainly come at the end of some years with a great army and much equipment.

14 'And in those times many shall rise up against the king of the South; also *certain* violent men of your people shall exalt themselves in fulfilment of the vision, but they shall fall.

15 'So the king of the North shall come and build a siege-mound, and take a fortified city; and the forces of the South shall not withstand *him*. Even his choice troops *shall have* no strength to resist.

16 'But he who comes against him shall do according to his own will, and no one shall stand against him. He shall stand in the Glorious Land with destruction in his power.

17 'He shall also set his face to enter with the strength of his whole kingdom, and upright ones with him; thus shall he do. And he shall give him the daughter of women to destroy it; but she shall not stand *with him*, or be for him.

18 'After this he shall turn his face to the coastlands, and shall take many. But a ruler shall bring the reproach

and place there the abomination of desolation."'

The desolation referred to here must be that carried out by Ecclesiastical Rome when she obscured the ministry of our High Priest in the heavenly sanctuary.

40 '"At the time of the end . . . . "''
45 '"He shall plant the tents of his palace between the seas and the glorious holy mountain."''

This part of the prophecy yet awaits fulfilment, and could mean that the Papacy would remove its headquarters to Jerusalem.

CHRIST

Daniel 12:1 '"At that time Michael shall stand up, the great prince . . . of your people."''

The expression 'to stand up' is used consistently throughout chapter eleven to mean that a king begins to reign. In this verse it must mean that Jesus, having completed His priestly ministry, receives the kingdom from His Father, the Ancient of Days, and prepares to return to earth to take His people home.

'"And there shall be a time of trouble . . . . And at that time your people shall be delivered, every one who is found written in the book."''

The time of trouble would be the plagues described in Revelation 16. The verdict of the Ancient of Days '"in favour of the saints"''

against them to an end; and with the reproach removed, he shall turn back on him.

19 'Then he shall turn his face towards the fortress of his own land; but he shall stumble and fall, and not be found.

20 'There shall arise in his place one who imposes taxes *on* the glorious kingdom; but within a few days he shall be destroyed, but not in anger or in battle.

21 'And in his place shall arise a vile person, to whom they will not give the honour of royalty; but he shall come in peaceably, and seize the kingdom by intrigue.

22 'With the force of a flood they shall be swept away from before him and be broken, and also the prince of the covenant.

23 'And after the league *is made* with him he shall act deceitfully, for he shall come up and become strong with a small *number* of people.

24 'He shall enter peaceably, even into the richest places of the province; and he shall do *what* his fathers have not done, nor his forefathers: he shall disperse among them the plunder, spoil, and riches; and he shall devise his plans against the strongholds, but *only* for a time.

25 'He shall stir up his power and his courage against the king of the South with a great army. And the king of the south shall be stirred up to battle with a very great and mighty army; but he shall not stand, for they shall devise plans against him.

26 'Yes, those who eat of the portion of his delicacies shall destroy him; his army shall be swept away, and many shall fall down slain.

27 'Both these kings' hearts *shall be* bent on evil, and they shall speak lies at the same table; but it shall not prosper, for the end *will* still *be* at the appointed time.

28 'While returning to his land with great riches, his heart shall be *moved* against the holy covenant; so he shall do *damage* and return to his own land.

(Dan. 7:22), would ensure that one's name is safely included in the Book of Life. The importance of this book is further developed in Revelation 3:5; 20:15 and 21:27.

WORDS RESERVED FOR US

12:4 '"But you, Daniel, shut up the words, and seal the book until the time of the end; many shall run to and fro, and knowledge shall increase."'

Thus Daniel received the assurance that knowledge of his words would increase in the latter days. As men would run to and fro through his book, trying to understand its message, understanding would come to them. But when?

6, 7 '"How long shall the fulfilment of these wonders be?" . . . It shall be for a time, times, and half a time.'

Not until the end of the papal supremacy in 1798 would Daniel's prediction be fully understood. Thus it proved. Only twenty books a century from the introduction of printing onwards were published explaining the book of Daniel. But after the year 1800 more than a hundred books on Daniel were published in the first fifty years. What must the figure be now!

9, 13 '"Go your way, Daniel, for the words are closed up and sealed till the time of the end. . . . But you . . . shall rest, and will arise to your inheritance at the end of the days."'

29 'At the appointed time he shall return and go towards the south; but it shall not be like the former or the latter.

30 'For ships from Cyprus shall come against him; therefore he shall be grieved, and return in rage against the holy covenant, and do *damage*. So he shall return and show regard for those who forsake the holy covenant.

31 'And forces shall be mustered by him, and they shall defile the sanctuary fortress; then they shall take away the daily *sacrifices*, and place *there* the abomination of desolation.

32 'Those who do wickedly against the covenant he shall corrupt with flattery; but the people who know their God shall be strong, and carry out *great exploits*.

33 'And those of the people who understand shall instruct many; yet *for many* days they shall fall by sword and flame, by captivity and plundering.

34 'Now when they fall, they shall be aided with a little help; but many shall join with them by intrigue.

35 'And *some* of those of understanding shall fall, to refine them, purge *them*, and make *them* white, *until* the time of the end; because *it is* still for the appointed time.

36 'Then the king shall do according to his own will: he shall exalt and magnify himself above every god, shall speak blasphemies against the God of gods, and shall prosper till the wrath has been accomplished; for what has been determined shall be done.

37 'He shall regard neither the God of his fathers nor the desire of women, nor regard any god; for he shall magnify himself above *them* all.

38 'But in their place he shall honour a god of fortresses; and a god which his fathers did not know he shall honour with gold and silver, with precious stones and pleasant things.

39 'Thus he shall act against the strongest fortresses with a foreign god, which he shall acknowledge, *and* advance *its* glory; and he shall cause them to rule over many, and divide the land for gain.

And so it is. Daniel has come into his own. Even what was mysterious to Daniel himself, especially the long periods involved, are now clear to us who can look back on the long history he covered. Jesus' statement about the purpose of inspired predictions has come true for Daniel's words as well as for His own: "'I have told you before it comes, that when it does come to pass, you may believe.'" (John 14:29.) And there are other words from Jesus.

Revelation 1:1, 3 'The Revelation of Jesus Christ .... he sent and signified it by his angel to his servant John .... Blessed is he who reads and those who hear the words of this prophecy, and keep those things which are written in it.'

In the Book of Revelation, the last book in our Bibles, the apostle John takes up the very topics discussed in the book of Daniel. In chapters 12 to 14 John deals with the period of three-and-a-half times in Daniel's account of the beasts and the saints, and announces the very time of the opening of that judgement that is described in Daniel 7. In Revelation 15 and 16 he introduces the final activities proceeding from the sanctuary spoken of in Daniel 8 and 9. In Revelation 17 to 20 John begins where Daniel left off in chapter 12 — the standing up of Michael to begin His reign. Revelation 21

40 'At the time of the end the king of the South shall attack him; and the king of the North shall come against him like a whirlwind, with chariots, horsemen, and with many ships; and he shall enter the countries, overwhelm *them*, and pass through.
41 'He shall also enter the Glorious Land, and many *countries* shall be overthrown; but these shall escape from his hand: Edom, Moab, and the prominent people of Ammon.
42 'He shall stretch out his hand against the countries, and the land of Egypt shall not escape.
43 'He shall have power over the treasures of gold and silver, and over all the precious things of Egypt; also the Libyans and Ethiopians *shall follow* at his heels.
44 'But news from the east and the north shall trouble him; therefore he shall go out with great fury to destroy and annihilate many.
45 'And he shall plant the tents of his palace between the seas and the glorious holy mountain; yet he shall come to his end, and no one will help him.

12 'At that time Michael shall stand up,
The great prince who stands *watch* over the sons of your people;
And there shall be a time of trouble,
Such as never was since there was a nation,
Even to that time.
And at that time your people shall be delivered,
Every one who is found written in the book.
2 And many of those who sleep in the dust of the earth shall awake,
Some to everlasting life,
Some to shame *and* everlasting contempt.
3 Those who are wise shall shine
Like the brightness of the firmament,
And those who turn many to righteousness

49

and 22 describe in glorious detail the kingdom of God that was but barely introduced at the end of the king's dream in Daniel 2. To these 'end-time' visions we must now turn. They were never sealed. Quite the opposite, they are a 'revelation', opening before our eyes the constant care of God for those in a troubled world who are loyal to Him.

Like the stars for ever and ever.

4 'But you, Daniel, shut up the words, and seal the book until the time of the end; many shall run to and fro, and knowledge shall increase.'

5 Then I, Daniel, looked; and there stood two others, one on this river-bank and the other on that river-bank.

6 And *one* said to the man clothed in linen, who *was* above the waters of the river, 'How long shall the fulfilment of these wonders *be?*'

7 Then I heard the man clothed in linen, who *was* above the waters of the river, when he held up his right hand and his left hand to heaven, and swore by him who lives for ever, that *it shall be* for a time, times, and half *a time;* and when the power of the holy people has been completely shattered, all these *things* shall be finished.

8 Although I heard, I did not understand. Then I said, 'My Lord, what *shall be* the end of these *things?*'

9 And he said, 'Go *your way*, Daniel, for the words *are* closed up and sealed till the time of the end.

10 'Many shall be purified, made white, and refined, but the wicked shall do wickedly; and none of the wicked shall understand, but the wise shall understand.

11 'And from the time *that* the daily *sacrifice* is taken away, and the abomination of desolation is set up, *there shall be* one thousand two hundred and ninety days.

12 'Blessed *is* he who waits, and comes to the one thousand three hundred and thirty-five days.

13 'But you, go *your way* till the end; for you shall rest, and will arise to your inheritance at the end of the days.'

REVIEW

1 *Was the angel's account of the kings who would immediately follow Cyrus proved correct by history?*

2 *Why do the next ten verses give us details of only two of the four divisions of Alexander's empire?*

3 *Who must be the rulers that occupy the rest of the chapter? Why do you think so?*

4 *What is the meaning of the expression 'Michael shall stand up'?*

5 *How are those described who will be delivered in the time of trouble?*

6 *At what time did Gabriel say knowledge would increase? And what, according to the context, would this be knowledge of?*

7 *According to Jesus, for what purpose are divine predictions given us?*

Oppression reaches its climax

THE CHURCH A WOMAN

Revelation 12:1 'A woman clothed with the sun . . . the moon . . . a garland of twelve stars.'

God's people, in both Testaments, are spoken of as betrothed or married to the Lord. (Isa. 54:5; Hosea 2:19; 2 Cor. 11:2.) The twelve apostles in the NT are the equivalent of the twelve tribes in the OT. (Gen. 49:28; Luke 6:12, 13; 22:29, 30.)

5 'She bore a male child who was to rule all nations with a rod of iron.'

Israel had long looked forward to the arrival of the Messianic King who would rule with a rod of iron. (Ps. 2:7-12; Micah 5:2, 3; Rev. 19:15, 16.)

3 'A great, fiery red dragon having seven heads and . . . seven diadems on his heads.'

As the self-appointed ruler of this world (Luke 4:5, 6), and so recognized by Jesus, (John 12:31 and 14:30), the devil has ruled through human governments wherever possible. From the beginning of Israel's national history, he has oppressed the people of God, and will continue to do so until the end of the age. The seven oppressive govern-

REVELATION 12 – 14

12 Now a great sign appeared in heaven: a woman clothed with the sun, with the moon under her feet, and on her head a garland of twelve stars.

2 Then being with child, she cried out in labour and in pain to give birth.

3 And another sign appeared in heaven: behold, a great, fiery red dragon having seven heads and ten horns, and seven diadems on his heads.

4 His tail drew a third of the stars of heaven and threw them to the earth. And the dragon stood before the woman who was ready to give birth, to devour her child as soon as it was born.

5 And she bore a male child who was to rule all nations with a rod of iron. And her child was caught up to God and *to* his throne.

6 Then the woman fled into the wilderness, where she has a place prepared by God, that they should feed her there one thousand two hundred and sixty days.

7 And war broke out in heaven: Michael and his angels fought against the dragon; and the dragon and his angels fought,

8 but they did not prevail, nor was a place found for them in heaven any longer.

9 So the great dragon was cast out, that serpent of old, called the Devil and Satan, who deceives the whole world; he was cast to the earth, and his angels were cast out with him.

10 Then I heard a loud voice saying in heaven, 'Now salvation, and strength, and the kingdom of our God, and the power of his Christ have come, for the accuser of our brethren, who accused them before our God day and night, has been cast down.

ments would be: Egypt (Exod. 1:5); Assyria (Isa. 52:4; 2 Kings 17:6); Babylon (2 Kings 25:8-12); Persia (Esther 3:8-13); Greece (1 Macc. 1); Imperial Rome, in power at the time of this prophecy (John 19:15); and Ecclesiastical Rome, 'not yet come' in the time of John. (Rev. 17:10; Dan. 7:25.)

'And ten horns.'

The ten horns must be the same as those mentioned by Daniel, the governments of Europe contemporaneous with the Papacy. (Dan. 7:24; Rev. 17:12, 13.) At the time of the birth of Christ, the sixth head, Imperial Rome, was ruling the world. (Luke 2:1.) Hence at the time of the events portrayed in these verses, the diadems are seen on the heads. In the next vision, referring to events which would take place later, the diadems will be seen on the horns. (Rev. 13:1.)

4 'His tail drew a third of the stars of heaven and threw them to the earth.'

The first interpretation of 'stars' given in this book is 'angels'. (Rev. 1:20.) The devil persuaded a large portion of the angels of heaven to follow him in his rebellion, and so they were thrown out of heaven with him. (Rev. 12:9.)

'The dragon stood . . . to devour her child as soon as it was born.'

Herod's attempt to slay the

11 'And they overcame him by the blood of the Lamb and by the word of their testimony, and they did not love their lives to the death.

12 'Therefore rejoice, O heavens, and you who dwell in them! Woe to the inhabitants of the earth and the sea! For the devil has come down to you, having great wrath, because he knows that he has a short time.'

13 Now when the dragon saw that he had been cast to the earth, he persecuted the woman who gave birth to the male *child*.

14 But the woman was given two wings of a great eagle, that she might fly into the wilderness to her place, where she is nourished for a time and times and half a time, from the presence of the serpent.

15 So the serpent spewed water out of his mouth like a flood after the woman, that he might cause her to be carried away by the flood.

16 But the earth helped the woman, and the earth opened its mouth and swallowed up the flood which the dragon had spewed out of his mouth.

17 And the dragon was enraged with the woman, and he went to make war with the rest of her offspring, who keep the commandments of God and have the testimony of Jesus Christ.

13 Then I stood on the sand of the sea. And I saw a beast rising up out of the sea, having seven heads and ten horns, and on his horns ten crowns, and on his heads a blasphemous name.

2 Now the beast which I saw was like a leopard, his feet were like *the feet of* a bear, and his mouth like the mouth of a lion. And the dragon gave him his power, his throne, and great authority.

3 I saw one of his heads as if it had been mortally wounded, and his deadly wound was healed. And all the world marvelled and followed the beast.

4 So they worshipped the dragon who gave authority to the beast; and they worshipped the beast, saying, 'Who *is*

Child of Bethlehem was doubtless devil-inspired. (Matt. 2:13-16.) Many were the later attempts to kill Jesus, and eventually it seemed that they were successful. (John 5:18; 10:31, 39; 11:53; Acts 4:26, 27.)

5 *'Her child was caught up to God and to his throne.'*

The devil killed Him, but did not devour Him. Instead, by dying He conquered the devil. (Heb. 2:14.) Then He ascended to await the final fall of all His enemies. (Heb. 10:12, 13.)

6 *'The woman fled into the wilderness.'*

The experience of the church summarized in this verse is expanded in verses 13 to 17. Meanwhile the prophet is shown the deeper meaning of these events by being given a view behind the scenes.

THE COSMIC CONFLICT

7 *'War broke out in heaven.'*

As redemption through the Lamb was planned 'before the foundation of the world' (1 Peter 1:18-20; 2 Tim. 1:9), the origin of evil must have occurred before the world began. Hence it was immediately after creation that 'that serpent of old' appeared in the Garden and began his deceptions. (Gen. 3:4, 5.) Since then, not only Job, but many others also have suffered from his

like the beast? Who is able to make war with him?'

5 And he was given a mouth speaking great things and blasphemies, and he was given authority to continue *for* forty-two months.

6 Then he opened his mouth in blasphemy against God, to blaspheme his name, his tabernacle, and those who dwell in heaven.

7 And it was granted to him to make war with the saints and to overcome them. And he was given authority over every tribe, tongue, and nation.

8 And all who dwell on the earth will worship him, whose names have not been written in the book of life of the Lamb slain from the foundation of the world.

9 If anyone has an ear, let him hear.

10 He who leads into captivity shall go into captivity; he who kills with the sword must be killed with the sword. Here is the patience and the faith of the saints.

11 Then I saw another beast coming up out of the earth, and he had two horns like a lamb and spoke like a dragon.

12 And he exercises all the authority of the first beast in his presence, and causes the earth and those who dwell in it to worship the first beast, whose deadly wound was healed.

13 He performs great signs, so that he even makes fire come down from heaven on the earth in the sight of men.

14 And he deceives those who dwell on the earth by those signs which he was granted to do in the sight of the beast, telling those who dwell on the earth to make an image to the beast who was wounded by the sword and lived.

15 He was granted *power* to give breath to the image of the beast, that the image of the beast should both speak and cause as many as would not worship the image of the beast to be killed.

16 And he causes all, both small and great, rich and poor, free and slave, to

accusations'. (Job 1:9-11.) The prophet Isaiah, when shown the evil spirit then operating through the king of Babylon, the third diadem the dragon wore, was given to understand the self-exalting aspirations of Lucifer that brought about his downfall. (Isa. 14:12-15.)

'Michael and his angels fought.'

The name 'Michael' means 'he who is like God'. Jesus is 'the express image of his (Father's) person.' (Heb. 1:3.) He created the angels. (Col. 1:16.) He is therefore their commander or 'archangel'. It is the archangel's voice that raises the dead. (1 Thess. 4:16.) Jesus said that it is He Himself who will raise the dead. (John 5:28, 29.) He is that 'Michael the archangel' who disputed with the devil over (the raising of) the body of Moses. (Jude 9.) He is already known to us through Daniel as the leader and protector of His loyal servants on the earth. (Dan. 10:21; 12:1.)

9 *'The great dragon was cast out . . . and his angels were cast out with him.'*

The presence and activity of evil angels have been all too evident in the temptations that have pressed on humanity since our first parents succumbed to temptation. But Christ's ascension after rising from the dead is the great turning point in the conflict.

receive a mark on their right hand or on their foreheads,

17 and that no one may buy or sell except one who has the mark or the name of the beast, or the number of his name.

18 Here is wisdom. Let him who has understanding calculate the number of the beast, for it is the number of a man: His number *is* 666.

14 Then I looked, and behold, a Lamb standing on Mount Zion, and with him one hundred *and* forty-four thousand, having his Father's name written on their foreheads.

2 And I heard a voice from heaven, like the voice of many waters, and like the voice of loud thunder. And I heard the sound of harpists playing their harps.

3 And they sang as it were a new song before the throne, before the four living creatures, and the elders; and no one could learn that song except the hundred *and* forty-four thousand who were redeemed from the earth.

4 These are the ones who were not defiled with women, for they are virgins. These are the ones who follow the Lamb wherever he goes. These were redeemed from *among* men, *being* first-fruits to God and to the Lamb.

5 And in their mouth was found no guile, for they are without fault before the throne of God.

6 Then I saw another angel flying in the midst of heaven, having the everlasting gospel to preach to those who dwell on the earth — to every nation, tribe, tongue, and people —

7 saying with a loud voice, 'Fear God and give glory to him, for the hour of his judgment has come; and worship him who made heaven and earth, the sea and springs of water.'

8 And another angel followed, saying, 'Babylon is fallen, is fallen, that great city, because she has made all nations drink of the wine of the wrath of her fornication.'

9 Then a third angel followed them,

10 *'"Now ... the power of his Christ have come, for the accuser ... has been cast down."'*

God had permitted His Son to come into the world where Satan claimed dominion, to suffer under his murderous efforts from the manger to the cross. The contrast was such that the affections of the angels in heaven were effectually uprooted from Satan. No longer would they be influenced by his 'accusations'. (John 12:31-33.) Jesus had entered the strong man's house and overcome him. (Luke 11:20-22; Heb. 2:14, 15.)

11 *'"They overcame him by the blood of the Lamb and by the word of their testimony."'*

When Jesus cried out from the cross, '"It is finished"', the redemption of man from the power of Satan was assured. (John 19:30.) We can have victory over Satan, not without the blood of the Lamb, and not without our own positive attitude and testimony.

12 *'"Woe to the inhabitants of the earth .... For the devil ... knows that he has (but) a short time."'*

As Satan's time grows shorter, and his end more certain, he increases the tempo of his deceit and destruction. His increasing efforts are brought to view in the following verses, the climax being reached in the 'war' mentioned in verse 17. That war is

saying with a loud voice, 'If anyone worships the beast and his image, and receives *his* mark on his forehead or on his hand,

10 'he himself shall also drink of the wine of the wrath of God, which is poured out full strength into the cup of his indignation. And he shall be tormented with fire and brimstone in the presence of the holy angels and in the presence of the Lamb.

11 'And the smoke of their torment ascends for ever and ever; and they have no rest day or night, who worship the beast and his image, and whoever receives the mark of his name.'

12 Here is the patience of the saints; here *are* those who keep the commandments of God and the faith of Jesus.

13 Then I heard a voice from heaven saying to me, 'Write: "Blessed *are* the dead who die in the Lord from now on."' 'Yes,' says the Spirit, 'that they may rest from their labours, and their works follow them.'

14 And I looked, and behold, a white cloud, and on the cloud sat *one* like the Son of Man, having on his head a golden crown, and in his hand a sharp sickle.

15 And another angel came out of the temple, crying with a loud voice to him who sat on the cloud, 'Thrust in your sickle and reap, for the time has come for you to reap, for the harvest of the earth is ripe.'

16 So he who sat on the cloud thrust in his sickle on the earth, and the earth was reaped.

17 Then another angel came out of the temple which is in heaven, he also having a sharp sickle.

18 And another angel came out from the altar, who had power over fire, and he cried with a loud cry to him who had the sharp sickle, saying, 'Thrust in your sharp sickle and gather the clusters of the vine of the earth, for her grapes are fully ripe.'

19 So the angel thrust his sickle into the earth and gathered the vine of the earth, and threw *it* into the great

described in greater detail in the accounts given in the next chapters.

winepress of the wrath of God.

20 And the winepress was trampled outside the city, and blood came out of the winepress, up to the horses' bridles, for one thousand six hundred furlongs.

THE CHURCH PERSECUTED

13 'The dragon . . . persecuted the woman who gave birth to the male child.'

Not admitting defeat, the devil carried on his war against Christ by concentrating his efforts on those who were loyal to Jesus.

14 'But the woman . . . is nourished for a time and times and half a time, from the presence of the serpent.'

The same period of time, called in verse 6 'one thousand two hundred and sixty days', familiar to us from Daniel 7:25 as a period of persecution, is now presented to us also as a period of divine protection.

15 'The serpent spewed water out of his mouth like a flood after the woman.'

This familiar symbol for invading armies (Isa. 8:7; Jer. 46:8), here refers to that flood of crusades, dragonnades, invading armies, and inquisitors, poured out upon dissenters during medieval times.

16 'But the earth helped the woman . . . and swallowed up the flood.'

Christian believers in Scotland and Ireland did not come under the control of Roman priests until about AD 700. Remarkably they were comparatively free from interference even in northern Italy and in Switzerland up to about AD 1200. After the Reformation, Protestants found temporary refuge in Sweden, England and Holland, but real relief came when those seeking civil and religious liberty were able to escape to the New Word. Twenty thousand refugees settled in New England in the twenty years between 1620 and 1640, and in that country established the beginning of a free nation destined to grow into a powerful confederation of states by the continued immigration of those who sought relief from oppression.

17 'The dragon . . . went to make war with the rest of her offspring.'

'The rest of her offspring are those who survived the efforts of the dragon to destroy them. This group is better known in the translation 'the remnant of her seed', and 'the remnant' is a theme familiar to Bible readers. The dragon, under his Assyrian head, attempted to destroy the people of God in the days of Hezekiah, carrying Israel away, and invading Judah, but a remnant survived. (2 Chron. 30:6.) Under his Babylonian head, the dragon seemed to have finally succeeded when he carried Judah back to the land Abraham came from, but a remnant returned to Judea and began again. (Ezra 9:14, 15.) But there is something worse than physical death. It is loss of spiritual life. In the days of the imperial Roman head, the apostle Paul, recalling an earlier group of faithful ones, recognized that the small number of Christian believers among the Jews were a righteous remnant. (Rom. 11:5.) So, as John sees the efforts of the dragon under the seventh head, he is encouraged to know that there will be a remnant who are faithful to God. He has already been told of the 144,000 'servants of the living God', and after this final onslaught of 'war' by the dragon has taken place, he will be shown that they will have survived. (Rev. 7:1-4; 14:1-5.) They will survive because they —

'Keep the commandments of God.'

It is the devil who tempts mankind to sin. Sin is the transgression of God's law. (1 John 3:4.) Jesus came to save us from sin. (Matt. 1:21.) The first step in receiving salvation is repentance from sinning. (Acts 2:37, 38; 20:20, 21.) Obedience to God cannot be disregarded if one would live in the presence of God. (Matt. 7:21.) The servants of God keep the commandments of God. (Rev. 14:12.) Such obedience would include the fourth commandment as well as the other nine. (James 1:12, 22; 2:10-12.)

'And [they] have the testimony of Jesus.'

Some Bible translations render this expression as bearing 'witness to Jesus'. The Greek phrase here used by John can grammatically mean either testimony 'to' Jesus or testimony 'from' Jesus. However, in the book of Revelation where this phrase is used the context makes it plain that we must understand it to mean the testimony that Jesus sends us through the prophets inspired by His Spirit. (Rev. 1:1, 2; 19:10; 1 Peter 1:11.) John is being assured that the faithful ones who observe all of God's commands will be favoured with a further knowledge of God's will through the messages He would send them by means of the gift of prophecy.

In the ten years after the year 1844, those who were looking for the Advent spent much time in a renewed study of the Scriptures. As a result they began to keep the Sabbath. And to them came the added blessing of the 'testimony of Jesus' through the visions received by Ellen White. During the seventy years of her faithful ministry she received some two thousand visions. Her writings have been a lesser light that has constantly pointed to the greater light of the Bible. Her writings encourage Bible study, promote personal religious experience, give practical counsel to parents, to youth, to pastors and evangelists, and have been the guiding light behind the worldwide educational, missionary, publishing, and humanitarian work of Seventh-day Adventists.

THE BEAST ON THE DRAGON'S THRONE

Revelation 13:1 'A beast rising up out of the sea.'

This beast, who resembles Daniel's four beasts in other ways, arose like them from the surging sea of earth's peoples. So Ecclesiastical Rome arose to prominence during the tribal movements which occurred during and after the fall of the Western Roman Empire.

'Having seven heads and ten horns, and on his horns ten crowns.'

Imperial Rome has passed away, and the crowns are on the kings of Europe during Rome's ecclesiastical phase. Thus we have arrived at the time of the authority of the seventh head.

2 'The beast . . . I saw was like a leopard . . . a bear . . . a lion.'

• The leopard's influence on the medieval Papacy may be seen in her whole scholastic theology for it was based on Greek philosophy. It may be seen also in her doctrine of natural immortality which she received from the Greeks.
• The influence of the Persian bear is evident in her asceticism and monasticism, for they reproduce the Persian

doctrine of dualism between matter and spirit. Persian influence was also exercised through her warrior god Mithras, which attracted the Roman soldiers who served in the east, and whose worship was brought back by them and even promoted by emperors. This made it easy for the Church to exalt the Day of the Sun in place of the Bible Sabbath. • The lion Babylon was noted for the influence of its priests. Not more completely did the priests of Babylon rule over every phase of life in the city, than did the hierarchy of priests, prelates and Pope rule the life of Europe from the hovels of the peasants to the palaces of kings for hundreds of years.

'And the dragon gave him his power, this throne, and great authority.'

To the Papacy was given, and by the Papacy was eagerly accepted, that glory and power of the kingdoms of the world which the devil offered to Jesus. (Luke 4:5-8.) The temptation our Lord so nobly resisted in order to bring blessing to the world, was embraced by the bishops of Rome. Other Christian Churches existed in the early centuries, and still exist, for instance, the Greek Orthodox, the Coptic Church of Egypt and Ethiopia, the Armenian Church, and others. But when the western emperor abdicated in AD 476, the bishop of Rome to a large extent inherited what was left of the power, throne and authority of Caesar. The Holy Catholic and Apostolic Church of Rome, to use its full title, became the seventh representative of the dragon. From this verse onward it is called 'the beast'. It meets its end in Revelation 19:20.

3 'I saw one of its heads as if it had been mortally wounded.'

The wound of the Papacy, received when Pius VI was captured by the French in AD 1798, grew worse for a time. The Holy Roman Empire came to an end in 1806. The Congress of Vienna in 1815 ceded parts of the 16,000 square miles of the Papal States to three European Powers. In 1860 three quarters of the remainder were incorporated into the kingdom of Italy. Finally, in 1870, the last remaining province, including the city of Rome itself, was absorbed into Italy, leaving the Pope, as he claimed, a virtual 'prisoner' in the Vatican.

'And his deadly wound was healed.'

The healing began in February 1929, when Benito Mussolini

signed the Lateran Pact with Cardinal Gasparri, who later became Pope. Since then, Vatican City, though only one-sixth of a square mile in extent, has been an independent State with a strongly-organized government. The Bishop of Rome is a king again. He is crowned with the words: 'Receive this Tiara of three crowns and know that you are the Father of princes and kings, the Governor of the earth, and Vicar of our Saviour Jesus Christ.'

'And all the world marvelled and followed the beast.'
The political influence of the Pope today may be seen in that many nations, more than a hundred of them, maintain an ambassador at the Vatican. He is not only a bishop at the head of a Church, he is a king, claiming political power and exercising it. When international conferences are called, the Pope always sends a representative, not as a mere observer, but as one appointed to take a part on equal terms with the other representatives of national governments.

4 'So they worshipped the dragon who gave authority to the beast; and they worshipped the beast, saying, "Who is like the beast? Who is able to make war with him?"'
This further increase in the influence of the Papacy is already on its way, but here we are forewarned that whatever subservience political powers may yet give to the Papacy, will in fact be a yielding to the authority of the dragon. The collapse of Communism in the late 1980s was achieved through the co-operation of Polish Pope John Paul II and the United States' president Ronald Reagan, a co-operation facilitated by key Roman Catholic personnel in both the CIA and the State Department.

5, 6 'He was given authority to continue for forty-two months . . . he opened his mouth in blasphemy against God . . . [and] his tabernacle.'
Here the prophet obviously reverts to a consideration of the general character and history of the Papacy, already familiar to us from Daniel. The 'forty-two months' is yet another representation of the period of the papal supremacy from 538 to 1798. The blasphemy against God and His tabernacle, already depicted by Daniel, and recognized by Paul as still future in his day (2 Thess. 2:3, 4) is now already a well-attested fact of history.

Long may be the night, but the morning comes. In God's mysterious providence the Papacy was permitted to persecute the saints, but the time was limited. When the period ended in 1798 the Pope went into captivity in France and died there two years later. However, the dragon is still to make war on the remnant, and the prophet will now be shown how this will come about.

THE BEAST THAT IS A FALSE PROPHET

11 '*Another beast coming up out of the earth.*'

Not out of the surging sea of the masses of humanity. Not by warlike conquest like all the kingdoms before it. This one comes up out of the wide spaces of the earth which had already given refuge to the oppressed.

'*He had two horns like a lamb and spoke like a dragon.*'

The lamb is a symbol of Christ, the dragon a symbol of Satan. Like a wolf in sheep's clothing this beast appears lamb-like but acts dragon-like. No wonder it is afterwards referred to simply as 'the false prophet'. (Rev. 16:13; 19:20.)

12 '*He exercises all the authority of the first beast . . . whose deadly wound was healed.*'

This makes two things clear. Being called a 'beast' this is a political power. Coming after the healing of the wound, it is to exercise its authority after the Papacy has recovered. How right John Wesley was when he wrote his *Notes on Revelation*, published in 1754, 'He is not yet come, though he cannot be far off.' The United States, that has grown up largely by settlement in the vast territories of the New World, declared her independence in 1776. The papal wound has been healing since 1929. The United States has been speaking to the world in a tone of authority since 1945.

'*And causes the earth and those who dwell in it to worship the first beast.*'

Freedom-loving America, once a leading Protestant country without an established Church, is going to lead the world to accept the authority of the bishop of Rome! It would once have seemed impossible, but things are changing. At the beginning of this century the Catholic Church in America was supported by gifts from other nations. Now, at the end of the century, American Catholics send more money to Rome than all the Catholics in the rest of the world put together.

The highest form of worship we can give to God is to obey His requirements. The most effective way for the United States to offer worship to the Vatican would be by bowing to and enforcing its requirements. And that the sure word of God is about to tell us she will do.

13, 14 'He performs great signs, so that he even makes fire come down from heaven . . . and he deceives those who dwell on the earth by those signs.'

Elijah, a true prophet of God, once called for fire from heaven as a sign to indicate who is the true God. (1 Kings 18:24, 37-39.) So those in power will fulfil the prediction of Jesus and show signs and wonders so deceptive that the very elect will be in danger of being taken in. (Matt. 24:24; 2 Thess. 2:9.) We may, therefore, expect to see genuine miraculous wonders take place, but if they are used to support what the Scriptures declare to be false, we shall be able to discern 'the false prophet'.

'Telling those who dwell on earth to make an image to the beast.'

The Image which the United States will prompt the inhabitants of the earth to make is to be a replica of the Papacy. The Papacy was essentially a religious organization that achieved its ends by obtaining the support of the civil authorities for the enforcement of its observances. It began like this. The bishops encouraged the Emperor Constantine early in the fourth century to close government offices and city workshops on Sundays so that people might attend services of worship. But the people went to the theatre and the circus instead. The Emperor Honorious was then petitioned by the Council of Carthage in AD 401 to enact a law closing circuses and theatres on Sundays. The desired law was eventually secured in 425. 'In this way,' remarked the historian Neander, 'the Church received help from the State for the furtherance of her ends.' It was about the same time that St Augustine advocated the theory that, in dealing with Donatist heretics, the infliction of pain by the 'rod of temporal suffering' was useful to bring men back to God and to incite them 'to attain the highest grade of religious development'. As Neander said, this leaning on the secular arm 'contained the germ of that whole system of spiritual despotism, of intolerance and persecution which ended in the tribunals of the Inquisition.' In this way the 'beast' was formed. To conceive that America, the 'land of the free', could ever adopt the same principles and become guilty of similar intolerance, would seem a very far-fetched idea. But the prophet evidently foresaw the calling into existence of just such an image or replica of the Papacy, for he went on to say —

15 'He was granted power to . . . cause as many as would not worship the image of the beast to be killed.'

This indicates that the United States, which in the first amendment of its Constitution says that 'Congress shall make no law respecting an establishment of religion, or prohibiting the free exercise thereof' will not only give power to a religious body, perhaps a union of Churches in the USA, perhaps the Religious Right or its equivalent, but will make it a capital crime not to carry out the requirements of this body. By thus uniting Church and State and sustaining religious usages by civil law the lamb-like beast will have begun to speak with the voice of a dragon. How could such a situation be brought about?

16 'He causes all . . . to receive a mark.'

Of all the practices about which the various denominations of Christians could agree to ask the help of the State, Sunday observance has already in times past been made a matter of legal enforcement. It was the Roman Church that initiated Sunday observance and still openly claims to have done so, as shown in our comments on Daniel 7:25. If people today should observe Sunday under pressure of legal enforcement, they would in effect be yielding to the authority of Rome. In this way the false prophet would succeed in bringing about what John foretold in verse 12, namely, the 'worship' of the first beast.

'A mark on their right hand or on their foreheads.'

It can hardly be expected that everyone will willingly accept such regimentation. Certainly some will be ready to embrace the requirement willingly, believing it to be a requirement of

God. Such would symbolically receive the mark in their foreheads. But others, only outwardly conforming to avoid the penalties involved, would receive the seal symbolically on the hand.

17 *'No one may buy or sell.'*

The prophet has already told us that obedience will eventually be enforced on pain of death. This step would naturally be preceded by the promulgation of the mark of homage. Next would come the enforcement under civil penalties to the extent of economic sanctions. One would expect the next step to be fines and imprisonment, and only as a last resort the death penalty. The Lord Jesus once said: ' "The time is coming that whoever kills you will think that he offers God service." ' (John 16:2.) It has happened in the past. It will happen again. Only this time the test will be universal, for verses 3 and 4 of Revelation 13 say that after the healing of the wound 'all the world' will worship the beast, and verse 12 says that the next beast will 'cause the earth and those what dwell in it to worship the first beast'. Who then will not come under the death decree?

'Except one who has the mark . . . the name . . . or the number of his name.'

We have already noted that some will willingly conform and others merely give outward conformity. Both of these groups will receive the 'mark'. Members of the Catholic Church would be safe for they already have 'the name of the beast'. The most safe would presumably be bishops and archbishops who represent and exercise the authority of the Church in the name of the Pope. They may perhaps be said to bear his 'number'.

18 *'The number of the beast . . . is the number of a man: His number is 666.'*

What man other than the Pope could this refer to? His most frequently used title today is Vicar of Jesus Christ. The Papacy used for three centuries a notorious forgery known as the Donation of Constantine, to maintain its deceitful claims to great possessions and power. In that Latin document the Pope's title appears in the form Vicar of the Son of God,

Vicarius Filii Dei. And as the letters of the Latin alphabet were used in those days as they are today, as numerals, it is possible to give a numerical value to any word or name.

THEY PASSED THE TEST

Revelation 14:1 'Behold, a Lamb standing on Mount Zion, and with him [those] having his Father's name written on their foreheads.'

Not the name of the beast, but their heavenly Father's name. Not merely on their hands but on their foreheads. The prophet will see them again in that beautiful future kingdom of God with the same royal insignia upon them. (Rev. 22:4.) This company has already been defined as 'servants of God' and as having 'the seal of the living God'. (Rev. 7:2-4.) The 'seal' of God's law is found in the fourth commandment. This only, of all the ten, brings to view both the name and the title of the Lawgiver. Sabbath observance has always been a testimony to one's allegiance to the Creator God. (Isa. 58:13; Exod. 20:8-11.) In the earliest Christian Church the pressure of persecution singled out those who obeyed God rather than men. (Acts 4:18, 19; 5:28, 29.) When in the future a substitute sabbath will be enforced and men receive the mark of allegiance to the beast, so those who faithfully observe the Sabbath of the Lord will be eligible to receive 'the seal of the living God', and be assured of divine approval, ownership, and protection. (Rev. 7:1-3.)

'One hundred and forty-four thousand.'

The 'seal' of God is a symbol. 'Forehead' is a symbol. 'Israel' is a symbol. (Gal. 3:27-29.) So this unique 'number' is also a symbol. Twelve tribes each having twelve princes leading a unit of one thousand (1 Sam. 18:12, 13; Rev. 7:3-8), will point to the perfection in the eyes of God of those who will stand 'without fault' before the throne of God, having been 'redeemed' from 'every nation, tribe, tongue and people'. (Rev. 14:4-6.)

2, 3 'I heard the sound of harpists playing . . . and they sang . . . and no one could learn that song except the hundred and forty-four thousand.'

They had passed through 'the great tribulation' (Rev. 7:14), that final 'war' on those who 'keep the commandments of God'. (Rev. 12:17.) Like the three Hebrew captives in ancient Babylon, they had faced death rather than worship an image under duress. No wonder they can sing a song that others could not sing.

4 'These are the ones who were not defiled with women.'

They have not been unfaithful to their covenant with God, an unfaithfulness represented in both Testaments by adultery. (James 4:4.) These are marked with the name of God instead of the name of the beast for the very reason that they have not consorted with the world.

'These are the ones who follow the Lamb wherever he goes.'

All the redeemed will have this privilege, but doubtless it will be a special pleasure to this company. Following Jesus begins here as a day-by-day experience. (Luke 9:23.) Its climax will be staying 'with Him' in the final battle with the beast. (Rev. 17:14.)

'These . . . redeemed . . . being first-fruits.'

The word is obviously not to be taken in a chronological sense, but as it came to mean in ancient Israel, that which is set apart and dedicated wholly to the Lord. In ancient times the first-fruits, whether of field, orchard, oil press, flock, or oven, were to be the first and best of each type of produce, and were separated from the great mass laid up for common use. This part was considered a holy offering. (Lev. 23:17, 20; Deut. 18:4; Neh. 10:35-37.) Christian believers in any age are a 'kind of first-fruits' separated from the mass of humanity who give no thought to God. (James 1:18.) In the time of the end, when others yield allegiance to worldly authorities, 'the redeemed' are a holy people, dedicated to God.

5 'In their mouth was found no guile, for they are without fault.'

These words state plainly what the symbolic language of the preceding verses imply. Stated another way, they have ' "washed their robes and made them white in the blood of the Lamb." ' (Rev. 7:14.)

   We should note that no one has the mark of the beast at the present time. *The dragon-lamb exists already. The agencies that will form the image of the beast may be in existence, but the image of the beast does not yet exist.* No identifying mark has been announced, no sanctions listed, no death penalty proclaimed. Christian believers must not be considered as having the mark of the beast because they are observing Sunday as a day of worship. Thousands observe it reverently, sincerely believing, in spite of the utter lack of Bible evidence, that the day on which Christ rose from the dead was divinely ordained to take the place of the seventh day of the week, the only day called the Lord's Day in the Scriptures. (Isa. 58:13; Exod. 20:8-11; John 1:1-3; Mark 2:28.)

Only when the issue of obedience to earthly authorities instead of obedience to God is forced upon the attention of all, will mankind have to make the vital decision for life or for death, like the three men facing the furnace in Babylon. Each of us will then show whether or not we 'live by every word of God' by choosing which name we will bear.

MESSAGES OF WARNING

6 'I saw another angel flying in the midst of heaven, having the everlasting gospel to preach . . . to every nation, tribe, tongue and people.'

As the Gospel was by the Lord committed to men, not to angels (Matt. 28:19, 20; Mark 16:15), this angel must represent a body of human messengers. Their world-wide message is the Gospel of salvation, but it is to be given with a particular emphasis.

7 'Saying with a loud voice, "Fear God . . . for the hour of his judgement has come.'

When the apostles first preached the Gospel they spoke of the Judgement as something to come in the future. (Acts 17:22, 31; 24:24, 25.) Now a different and vital phase of the plan of salvation has been reached. The Gospel must still be proclaimed, and that to everyone, but this time with the added urgency that the Judgement has already begun. And we live in that day.

After Daniel's prediction about the 1,260 years of papal supremacy came to a clearly recognized ending in the year 1798, his words were unsealed, and thoughtful students of the Bible began to look at Daniel's longer period, the 2,300 days till the sanctuary was to be cleansed. In Britain such men as Edward Irving, James Frere, William Faber, William Cunninghame and Joseph Wolff began to proclaim that the end of the age would be reached between 1843 and 1847. Their testimony reached its high point about 1835. Then in North America from 1831 onwards, William Miller and others began to preach the same message, and pinpointed the correct date for the ending of the 2,300 days as AD 1844. All of these preachers thought of the Judgement and the coming of Christ as being one and the same. They overlooked the fact that though at the Judgement in Daniel 7:9, 13 the Son of Man comes on the clouds, He does not then come to earth but to the Holy of Holies in the Heavenly Sanctuary. Those who studied Daniel more closely identified the Judgement of Daniel 7 with the Cleansing of the Sanctuary in Daniel 8, and understood that this Judgement must occur before the actual return of Christ, for at that time He will claim those who have been accounted worthy to stand before Him. (Luke 21:36.)

'Worship him who made heaven and earth.'

When Adventists realized that in preaching that the pre-advent judgement had begun in 1844, they had actually been preaching the Gospel in terms of the first angel's message of Revelation 14, this led them to study the angel's message more closely. In this way they came upon another 'present truth' (2 Peter 1:12), that must be emphasized at this stage in the preaching of the everlasting Gospel, namely, that the God to be worshipped is the Creator. As a result they began to observe the seventh-day Sabbath. They realized that however innocent the emphasis on the resurrection day, the observance of that day had eclipsed the heaven-appointed memorial day that points to the creation and the Creator. They therefore began to publish a paper called *The Advent Review and the Sabbath Herald*. That happened in 1850. By 1860 they adopted the denominational name, Seventh-day Adventists.

8 *'Another angel followed, saying, "Babylon is fallen . . . that great city."'*

Miller and his associates had been mistaken about the arrival of the kingdom, but so had the disciples of Jesus in their preaching. The preaching of the disciples brought many to listen to Jesus, and so the Millerite message had brought conversion and change of heart to thousands. In turning against that message the churches of America suffered a spiritual loss. The Protestant Churches in America had in some ways become like the Catholic Church which Luther and his companions had recognized as 'Babylon'. Having rejected the life-changing messages about the approaching end of the age, they had brought spiritual declension upon themselves. They had fallen. They too were 'Babylon'.

'"She had made all nations drink of the wine of the wrath of her fornications."'

The fornication mentioned is explained more specifically to be the alliances of Christian Churches with the rulers of the world. (Rev. 18:3.) In other words, it is the worldliness of the Churches that displeases God. This condition has existed for a long time, but it daily becomes more obvious.

9, 10 'Then a third angel followed them, saying with a loud voice, "If anyone worships the beast and his image, and receives his mark on his forehead or on his hand, he himself shall also drink of the wine of the wrath of God."'

This message from God is intended to warn mankind not to be cowed by the threat of civil penalties. The message urges hearers to consider the more serious consequences of suffering the undiluted wrath of God to be poured out in the seven last plagues. (Rev. 15:1; 16:1, 2.)

'"He shall be tormented with fire and brimstone in the presence . . . of the Lamb."'

This additional punishment is 'the second death', the final destruction of sin and sinners. (Rev. 20:10, 14; 21:8.)

11 '"The smoke of their torment ascends for ever and ever."'

The word here translated as 'ever' means a space of time, but it does not mean an infinite space of time like the English word. The parallel expression used to describe the fate of the land of Esau illustrates the meaning of the word very well for Edom is not still burning. (Isa. 34:9, 10.) The lake of fire will destroy sinners when the whole surface of the planet is purified of its moral and physical pollution. However long-continued it may prove to be, it cannot be 'everlasting' in the full sense of the word, for it is to be succeeded by the earth restored to its original condition as the home of the saved. (Rev. 20:11-15; 21:1; 2 Peter 3:10-13.)

12 'Here is the patience of the saints; here are those who keep the commandments of God and the faith of Jesus.'

To serve God in a revolted world has never been easy. It will grow more difficult as the dragon's time gets shorter. 'He that shall endure unto the end shall be saved.' The early Christian Gospel preached by Paul is still applicable, ' "repentance toward God and faith toward our Lord Jesus Christ." ' (Acts 20:20, 21.) Repentance means nothing if it does not lead to amendment of life, in other words, to full obedience to God. And full obedience is impossible unless we remain united to the Saviour by faith. (John 15:5.)

13 ' " 'Blessed are the dead who die in the Lord from now on.' " ' . . . "that they may rest from their labours, and their works follow them." '

To keep God's law in today's world will become more difficult under the control of false religion. Blessed will be those who escape the terrible stress of the final issues of choosing between the mark of the beast or the seal of God. Yet how can they be blessed who have so eagerly looked forward to seeing their Lord's return, if they were to die before He comes? From Revelation 1:7 we learn that there will be a special resurrection of 'those who pierced him' if they are to witness His return. Daniel 12:2 completes the picture. It speaks not of a general resurrection, but of a resurrection of 'many', 'some' to everlasting contempt, and 'some' to everlasting life. This special resurrection taking place before the general resurrection of the righteous at the second coming (1 Thess. 4:16), would enable those who die in the faith of the third angel's message to welcome the Saviour at His glorious appearing.

THE TWO HARVESTS

14 'Behold, a white cloud, and on the cloud sat one like the Son of Man.'

The Son of God who became the Son of Man will return with a cloud of angels. (Matt. 26:64; 16:27.) The crown on His head is not this time a royal diadem but a victor's trophy. He is returning as the Conqueror in the battle with the dragon. He is the final Victor in the great controversy with the devil.

15 'Another angel came out of the temple, crying with a loud voice to him that sat on the cloud, "Thrust in your sickle and reap . . . for the harvest of the earth is ripe."'

In His parable Jesus explained: He who sows the good seed is the Son of Man. The field is the world. The good seeds are the sons of the kingdom. . . . The harvest is the end of the world, and the reapers are angels. (Matt. 13:37-39; 24:31.) It is from the temple in heaven, where Jesus has served as His people's High Priest, that the direction of the harvesting comes. It is in that temple that the decision as to whose names are retained in the book of life takes place.

16 'So he who sat on the cloud thrust in his sickle on the earth, and the earth was reaped.'

Those who have died believing in Jesus will rise from the dead and will be taken along with the righteous living, to 'always be with the Lord'. (1 Thess. 4:16, 17.) Their place in the New Jerusalem is secure for their names have been written in the Lamb's book of life since the pre-advent judgement. (Dan. 7:22; 12:1; Rev. 21:27.)

17, 18 'Then another angel came out of the temple which is in heaven, he also having a sharp sickle. And another angel came out from the altar, . . . saying, "Thrust in your sharp sickle and gather the clusters of the vine of the earth, for her grapes are fully ripe."'

This angel is to destroy the wicked. He also proceeds from the heavenly sanctuary. It is the centre from which all that concerns human salvation proceeds, even the destruction of those who reject God's gracious offer. '"This is the condemnation, that the light has come into the world, and men loved darkness rather than light."' (John 3:19.) 'This is the testimony: that God has given us eternal life, and this life is in his Son. He who has the Son has life; he who does not have the Son of God does not have life.' (1 John 5:11, 12.)

19 'So the angel thrust his sickle into the earth and gathered the vine of the earth, and threw it into the great winepress of the wrath of God.'

As the harvest of grain represents the righteous to be received into the granaries of heaven, so the grapes in the winepress refer to the fate of the lost. The harvest must include all those believers living when Jesus comes as well as those who will be raised in the resurrection of the just. In the same way the full vintage must include, besides those who do not have the seal of God at the Advent, all those who will be raised in the second resurrection at the end of the millennium. (Rev. 20:5, 6.) And —

20 *'The winepress was trampled outside the city.'*
The command to gather the grapes comes from the sanctuary angel 'who has authority over fire'. After the second resurrection the hosts of the lost are gathered by Satan around the Holy City in a last desperate show of defiance. Then fire comes down and destroys them as they stand around the city. That fire cleanses the whole earth so that it can be remade into the dwelling of those who have proved loyal to God. (Rev. 20:9, 15; 2 Peter 3:10, 13.)

REVIEW

1 What seven successive governments has the devil used to oppress those who would be faithful to God?

2 Name the real opponents in this controversy.

3 Under which of the seven governments was the decisive battle of the great controversy fought out?

4 Under which of the seven were the people of God persecuted for more than twelve centuries?

5 In the final battle what would you judge from verse 17 will be the great point at issue?

6 According to the same verse, what source of encouragement and counsel has been provided for God's people?

7 For what reasons must the first beast in Revelation 13 be identified as the papal head of the dragon?

8 What are the historical facts about the wounding and recovery of the Papacy?

9 How do the place and time of the appearance of the second beast help us to identify it as the United States of America?

10 What kind of organization would be required if it is to be an image or replica of the Papacy?

11 What advice would you give to someone who hoped to belong to the 144,000, sealed as a servant of the living God?

12 Does anyone now living have the seal of God or the mark of the beast?

13 Comparing verses 6 and 12 in chapter 14, would you conclude that the Gospel must be an important ingredient in all three messages?

14 At what date did the judgement announced by the first angel begin?

15 What is meant by the 'fornication' mentioned in the second message?

16 In what way is the third message an answer to the political pressures forecast in Revelation 13:15-17?

1,260 years (days) of papal supremacy

AD 538	Period of papal dominance and persecution	AD 1798
Decree of Justinian		Pope imprisoned by Napoleon

Daniel 7:25 A time, times, and the dividing of time

Daniel 12:7 A time, times, and an half

Revelation 11:2 Forty and two months

Revelation 11:3 Twelve hundred and sixty days

Revelation 12:6 Twelve hundred and sixty days

Revelation 12:14 A time, and times, and half a time

Revelation 13:5 Forty and two months

7 The Sanctuary Ministry Completed

The preceding visions have taken us right through to the end of the great controversy, to the final destruction of sin a thousand years beyond the return of Jesus. The remaining visions of the book of Revelation fill in important developments in the closing up of the plan of salvation. The first is the close of human probation, the end of mankind's opportunity to accept salvation.

Revelation 15:1 'I saw . . . seven angels having the seven last plagues, for in them the wrath of God is complete.'

The wrath of God will here be directed against those who have oppressed His loyal people. Before Israel was delivered from the oppression of Egyptian slavery ten plagues fell on Egypt. The Israelites as well as the Egyptians suffered under the first three, but not under the last seven. (Exod. 7:19; 8:6, 17, 21, 22; 9:6, 26, etc.) The seven last plagues speak of punishment for some, but also of deliverance for others.

THE MINISTRY OF MERCY ENDS

2, 3 'I saw something like a sea of glass mingled with fire, and those

REVELATION 15 and 16

15 Then I saw another sign in heaven, great and marvellous: seven angels having the seven last plagues, for in them the wrath of God is complete.

2 And I saw *something* like a sea of glass mingled with fire, and those who have the victory over the beast, over his image and over his mark *and* over the number of his name, standing on the sea of glass, having harps of God.

3 And they sing the song of Moses, the servant of God, and the song of the Lamb, saying:

'Great and marvellous *are* your works, Lord God Almighty!

Just and true *are* your ways,

O King of the saints!

4 Who shall not fear you, O Lord, and glorify your name?

For *you* alone *are* holy.

For all nations shall come and worship before you,

For your judgments have been manifested.'

5 After these things I looked, and behold, the temple of the tabernacle of the testimony in heaven was opened.

6 And out of the temple came the seven angels having the seven plagues, clothed in pure bright linen, and having their chests girded with golden bands.

7 Then one of the four living creatures gave to the seven angels seven golden bowls full of the wrath of God who lives for ever and ever.

8 The temple was filled with smoke from the power of God and from his power, and no one was able to enter temple till the seven plagues of the seven angels were completed.

16 Then I heard a loud voice from the temple saying to the seven angels,

*who have the victory over the beast
... and his image and ... his mark
.... They sing the song of Moses ...
and the song of the Lamb, saying,
"Great and marvellous are your
works, Lord God Almighty! Just and
true are your ways."'*

The people sang the song of Moses after they had crossed the Red Sea and were safe from the pursuing Egyptian army. (Exod. 15:1-21.) The hundred and forty-four thousand will sing their new song after they have been delivered from the final war upon them by the dragon. (Rev. 14:3.) This happy scene is shown to the prophet before he is shown the terrifying scenes of the seven last plagues and the battle of Armageddon which ends them. This assures him, and us, that there will be some who escape. He sees them standing at the sapphire pavement before the divine throne which other prophets had glimpsed and found so hard to describe. (Exod. 24:10; Ezek. 1:22, 26.)

5-8 *'After these things I looked, and behold, the temple of the tabernacle of the testimony in heaven was opened. And out of the temple came the seven angels having the seven plagues. ... The temple was filled with ... the glory of God ... and no one was able to enter the temple till the seven plagues ... were completed.'*

This action comes from the inner sanctuary, from the very throne of God in the great original Holy of Holies. The 'testi-

'Go and pour out the bowls of the wrath of God on the earth.'

2 So the first went and poured out his bowl upon the earth, and a foul and loathsome sore came upon the men who had the mark of the beast and those who worshipped his image.

3 Then the second angel poured out his bowl on the sea, and it became blood as of a dead *man*; and every living creature in the sea died.

4 Then the third angel poured out his bowl on the rivers and springs of water, and they became blood.

5 And I heard the angel of the waters saying:

'You are righteous, O Lord,
The one who is and who was and who is to be,
  Because you have judged these things.

6 For they have shed the blood of saints and prophets,
And you have given them blood to drink.
For it is their just due.'

7 And I heard another from the altar saying, 'Even so, Lord God Almighty, true and righteous *are* your judgments.'

8 Then the fourth angel poured out his bowl on the sun, and power was given to him to scorch men with fire.

9 And men were scorched with great heat, and they blasphemed the name of God who has power over these plagues; and they did not repent and give him glory.

10 Then the fifth angel poured out his bowl on the throne of the beast, and his kingdom became full of darkness; and they gnawed their tongues because of the pain.

11 And they blasphemed the God of heaven because of their pains and their sores, and did not repent of their deeds.

12 Then the sixth angel poured out his bowl on the great river Euphrates, and its water was dried up, so that the way of the kings from the east might be prepared.

13 And I saw three unclean spirits like

mony' is the ten commandments kept in the Ark which was covered by the mercy seat above which the presence of God was often manifested. (Exod. 31:18; 40:10, 21.) In the Israelite tabernacle the service of the Most Holy Place occurred only once a year. Any Israelite who did not take seriously this annual cleansing service risked disfellowship or death. (Lev. 16:30, 34; 23:27-30.) In that service when the high priest had completed the work of cleansing the whole sanctuary, he went out and laid all responsibility for the confessed sins of Israel on the scapegoat that represented Satan. Then he appointed a man to lead the goat away and to burn the carcasses of the animals used in the ceremony. So when our Saviour, having completed His saving work as our priest, leaves the sanctuary, it is an angel that lays hold of Satan and binds him (Rev. 20:1, 2), and it is the angels with 'authority over fire' that come into action. (Rev. 14:16, 18; 16:7.) Perhaps we have not always realized that the extensive descriptions of the sanctuary service in the books of Moses have as much to say about the destroying fire of the justice of God as they have about the saving blood and acceptable incense of divine love.

frogs *coming* out of the mouth of the dragon, out of the mouth of the beast, and out of the mouth of the false prophet.

14 For they are spirits of demons, performing signs, *which* go out to the kings of the earth and of the whole world, to gather them to the battle of that great day of God Almighty.

15 'Behold, I am coming as a thief. Blessed *is* he who watches, and keeps his garments, lest he *should* walk naked and they see his shame.'

16 And they gathered them together to the place called in Hebrew, Armageddon.

17 Then the seventh angel poured out his bowl into the air, and a loud voice came out of the temple of heaven, from the throne, saying, 'It is done!'

18 And there were noises and thunderings and lightnings; and there was a great earthquake, such a mighty and great earthquake as had not occurred since men were on the earth.

19 Now the great city was divided into three parts, and the cities of the nations fell. And great Babylon was remembered before God, to give her the cup of the wine of the fierceness of his wrath.

20 Then every island fled away, and the mountains were not found.

21 And great hail from heaven fell upon men, *every hailstone* about the weight of a talent. And men blasphemed God because of the plague of the hail, since that plague was exceedingly great.

THE MINISTRY OF JUSTICE BEGINS

Revelation 16:1, 2 'Then I heard a loud voice from the temple saying to the seven angels, "Go and pour out the bowls of the wrath of God on the earth." So the first went . . . and a foul and loathsome sore came upon the men who had the mark of the beast and those who worshipped his image.'

When economic sanctions have been applied, and one cannot buy or sell unless one offers the worship of obedience, one accepts the mark. But then comes this strange affliction that no one in medical practice can find a cure for. And there are these people about, who did not unite with the majority, who are not suffering!

3 *'The second angel poured out his bowl upon the sea, and it became blood . . . and every living creature in the sea died.'*

A red tide struck some coasts a few years ago, and the beaches stank. Imagine what it will be like when all the beaches are affected! Will some people say that God is sending these punishments on account of the impiety of those who refuse to unite with others in this matter of religious observance? If so, the next step is to deal decisively with these nonconformists. Let the death penalty be agreed upon and a date set after which such people will no longer have the protection of the law. Then God can't blame us for their stubbornness.

4-6 *'Then the third angel poured out his bowl on the rivers and springs of water . . . . And I heard the angel of the waters saying: "You are righteous, O Lord . . . because you have judged these things. For they have shed the blood of saints . . . and you have given them blood to drink."'*

Nobody has been killed yet, just the date set. But it is the intention that brings guilt. What will people in the great cities do when their water supplies are contaminated? Every household would be affected. Bottled water and soft drinks will not last forever. Some sources of water must be left fit for use or no one would survive.

8, 9 *'Then the fourth angel poured out his bowl on the sun . . . . and men were scorched with great heat.'*

It may be hoped that this plague will not be universal. The previous one couldn't have been, and the next one is limited to the kingdom of the beast. But a heat wave is almost inescapable. In addition to sores and thirst it will be unbearable. Will it cause men to think?

10, 11 *'Then the fifth angel poured out his bowl on the throne of the beast, and his kingdom became full of darkness . . . . [Men] blasphemed the God of heaven because of their pains and their sores, and did not repent.'*

A supernatural darkness falling upon Vatican City, and perhaps farther abroad, will give men at the top cause to think. Surely the accumulation of trouble in the form of sores, thirst, heat, and now darkness, should bring some change of mind, but evidently not a dropping of the death decree. That date has almost arrived.

ARMAGEDDON

12-14 'Then the sixth angel poured out his bowl on the great river Euphrates, and its water was dried up, so that the way of the kings of the east might be prepared. . . . Three unclean spirits . . . out of the mouth of the dragon . . . the beast, and . . . the false prophet . . . go out to the kings of the earth . . . to gather them to the battle of the great day of God Almighty.'

In 539 BC the Euphrates was turned aside that soldiers could wade under the walls of Babylon and take it. In this way the kings of the east, Darius and Cyrus, became rulers of Babylon. (Isa. 41:2; 44:27-45:3; Dan. 5:30, 31; 1:21.) The water of the Euphrates represents the 'peoples, multitudes, nations and tongues' who support the city of Babylon. (Rev. 17:5, 15.) When the three powers controlling the policies of Babylon agree on the 'final solution', and persuade the kings to fight against God by setting a date to kill God's servants, they will dry up the support of the nations. The peoples of earth, suffering the plagues, will realize at last that they have gone too far. They will turn and vent their anger on Babylon itself. (Rev. 17:12-16.) Thus the way for Christ and His Father to come from the east and destroy their enemies is prepared. (Matt. 16:27; 26:64; Rev. 19:11-15; 2 Thess. 1:7-9.)

15, 16 '"Behold, I am coming as a thief. Blessed is he who watches, and keeps his garments . . . . And they gathered them together in a place called . . . Armageddon."'

This word is spoken as an encouragement to the faithful to keep their clothes washed and white in the blood of the Lamb. And still further encouragement, indeed assurance of victory, is given by the reference to a certain famous battle, long celebrated in a song which ends, '"Thus let all your enemies perish, O Lord."' (Judges 5:31.) In the battle thus celebrated, the oppression of the northern Canaanites was brought to an end at 'the waters of Megiddo' in an attack launched by divine direction from a mountain on the other side of the valley of the

Kishon from the town of Megiddo. (Judges 4:4-7, 15; 5:18, 19.) The word Armageddon which can be interpreted 'the mount of Megiddo' may here indicate this victory mountain. The important point for us is that we are always standing 'with him' who is coming to make His surprise victory. (Rev. 17:14.)

17 'Then the seventh angel poured out his bowl into the air, and a loud voice came out of the temple of heaven, from the throne, saying, "It is done!"'

Divine Providence chooses to make the hour appointed to liquidate those who have served Him the very hour of their complete deliverance. The moment set for the attack on those who refuse to worship the beast or his image by receiving his mark, is the moment the seventh plague begins. The beast and the false prophet, the deceived agents of the dragon, have chosen this moment for the gathered kings to attack the servants of God. That precipitates the battle of the great day of God. While others who have been threatened with death are praying for deliverance, their oppressors are stricken with sudden terror. In the midst of the terror and confusion, the word of the Lord is fulfilled: 'The rebuke of his people he will take away from all the earth. . . . And it will be said in that day: "Behold, this is our God; we have waited for him, . . . we will be glad and rejoice in His salvation."' (Isa. 25:8, 9.) The battle of Armageddon has begun.

18-21 'There were . . . thunderings and lightnings; and . . . a great earthquake . . . . The great city was divided into three parts . . . . And great Babylon was remembered before God . . . . And great hail from heaven fell upon men, every hailstone about the weight of a talent.'

Now everything is in confusion. Even the threefold conspiracy breaks down, and Babylon goes down with it. For God has stepped in. A talent weighed about 75 pounds, and these would cause more destruction in a city than any terrorist bombs. But this is not all. The prophet will be shown more. The breakup of the fragile alliances will be shown more fully in the next chapter. The ruin of Babylon will be described in more detail in Revelation 18. The battle itself, in which their Saviour will bring an utter end to the beast and the false prophet is outlined in Revelation 19:11-21.

REVIEW

1 Why should songs of victory be shown the prophet before the ordeals from which they celebrate escape?

2 How may we know that the ministry of mercy ends before the plagues begin?

3 List the first five plagues in order, and ask yourself how we may know that they are not universal.

4 What historical deliverances are brought to mind by the references to Euphrates and Megiddo?

5 Do you recognize that the action of the dragon, beast and false prophet bringing defeat upon themselves is the climax of their effort to kill those who will not worship as required?

6 Is this triple alliance to be shattered by human or by divine intervention?

8 Final conquests of the King of kings

THE GRAND ALLIANCE COLLAPSES

Revelation 17:1, 2 'One of the seven angels who had the seven bowls came and talked with me . . . "Come, I will show you the judgement of the great prostitute who sits on many waters, with whom the kings of the earth committed fornication, and the inhabitants of the earth were made drunk with the wine of her fornication."'

5 'And on her forehead a name was written: Mystery, Babylon the Great, the mother of prostitutes.'

18 '"The woman . . . is that great city which reigns over the kings of the earth."'

This is further information about the city to be destroyed under the seventh plague. The mother Church of the Middle Ages became corrupt through her alliances with power and wealth. Bishops and nobles often came from the same families. Governments were guided by the Church, and the Church went along with the leaders of the political and social world. Her worldly principles, called 'the wine of her fornication', so influenced the 'inhabitants of the world', that even her daughter Churches, the reformed Churches that separated from her, learned to depend on their

REVELATION 17:1 – 19:10

17 Then one of the seven angels who had the seven bowls came and talked with me, saying to me, 'Come, I will show you the judgment of the great prostitute who sits on many waters,

2 'with whom kings of the earth committed fornication, and the inhabitants of the earth were made drunk with the wine of her fornication.'

3 So he carried me away in the Spirit into the wilderness. And I saw a woman sitting on a scarlet beast *which was* full of names of blasphemy, having seven heads and ten horns.

4 The woman was arrayed in purple and scarlet, and adorned with gold and precious stones and pearls, having in her hand a golden cup full of abominations and the filthiness of her fornication.

5 And on her forehead a name *was* written:

MYSTERY,
BABYLON THE GREAT,
THE MOTHER OF PROSTITUTES
AND OF THE ABOMINATIONS
OF THE EARTH.

6 And I saw the woman, drunk with the blood of the saints and with the blood of the martyrs of Jesus. And when I saw her, I marvelled with great amazement.

7 But the angel said to me, 'Why did you marvel? I will tell the mystery of the woman and of the beast that carries her, which has the seven heads and the ten horns.

8 'The beast that you saw was, and is not, and will ascend out of the bottomless pit and go to perdition. And

relationships with government and society.

They also became prostitute. They also deserved the name 'Babylon'. Thus the way will be prepared for a religio-political set-up to be formed which will prove to be a replica of the Papacy, an 'image' of the 'beast'.

4-6 'The woman was arrayed in purple and scarlet, and adorned with gold . . . and pearls . . . . And on her forehead a name . . . Babylon . . . . And I saw the woman, drunk with the blood of the saints.'

15 ' "And the waters which you saw, where the prostitute sits, are peoples, multitudes, nations, and tongues." '

This gaudily-dressed woman, who has power over kings and peoples, and who persecutes, is in complete contrast to the persecuted woman in celestial garments, whose children are the Christ-child and those who keep the commandments. (Rev. 12:1, 2, 13, 17.) One represents the faithful people of God in all ages. The other must represent corrupt religion from the beginning of time. They are both associated with cities. One began as the tower of Babel on the Euphrates, built by men to make for themselves a name. (Gen. 11:1-9.) The other has no abiding city here, but looks forward to the Holy City which contains the river of life. (Rev. 21:9, 10; 22:1, 2.)

those who dwell on the earth will marvel, whose names are not written in the book of life from the foundation of the world, when they see the beast that was, and is not, and yet is.

9 'Here *is* the mind which has wisdom: The seven heads are seven mountains on which the woman sits.

10 'There are also seven kings. Five have fallen, one is, *and* the other has not yet come. And when he comes, he must continue a short time.

11 'And the beast that was, and is not, is himself also the eighth, and is of the seven, and is going to perdition.

12 'And the ten horns which you saw are ten kings who have received no kingdom as yet, but they receive authority for one hour as kings with the beast.

13 'These are of one mind, and they will give their power and authority to the beast.

14 'These will make war with the Lamb, and the Lamb will overcome them, for he is Lord of lords and King of kings; and those *who are* with him *are* called, chosen, and faithful.'

15 And he said to me, 'The waters which you saw, where the prostitute sits, are peoples, multitudes, nations, and tongues.

16 'And the ten horns which you saw on the beast, these will hate the prostitute, make her desolate and naked, eat her flesh and burn her with fire.

17 'For God has put it into their hearts to fulfil his purpose, to be of one mind, and to give their kingdom to the beast, until the words of God are fulfilled.

18 'And the woman whom you saw is that great city which reigns over the kings of the earth.'

18 After these things I saw another angel coming down from heaven, having great authority, and the earth was illuminated with his glory.

2 And he cried mightily with a loud voice, saying, 'Babylon the great is fallen, is fallen, and has become a

3 'I saw a woman sitting on a scarlet beast . . . having seven heads and ten horns.'

8 '"The beast that you saw was, and is not, and will ascend out of the bottomless pit."'

10, 11 '"There are seven kings. Five have fallen, one is, and the other has not yet come. And when he comes, he must continue a short time. And the beast that was, and is not, is himself the eighth, and is of the seven."'

The angel explains all this from the standpoint of John's own time. The five powers already fallen were Egypt, Assyria, Babylon, Persia and Greece. The one then reigning and even holding John a captive on the island of Patmos, was Imperial Rome. (Rev. 1:9.) The one 'not yet come' would prove to be the Papacy. The scarlet beast, though 'of the seven', would be 'the eighth'. This can be no other than the revived Papacy even now ruling as a political power in Vatican City.

12, 13 '"The ten horns . . . are ten kings who have received no kingdom as yet . . . . These are of one mind, and they will give their power and authority to the beast."'

18 '"And the woman . . . reigns over the kings of the earth."'

The woman is said to be carried by the beast and reign over the kings. The scarlet beast and the scarlet woman together make one religio-political entity, as did Daniel's fourth beast and little horn. This was the situation in medieval times under the seventh

habitation of demons, a prison for every foul spirit, and a cage for every unclean and hated bird!

3 'For all the nations have drunk of the wine of the wrath of her fornication, the kings of the earth have committed fornication with her, and the merchants of the earth have become rich through the abundance of her luxury.'

4 And I heard another voice from heaven saying, 'Come out of her, my people, lest you share in her sins, and lest you receive of her plagues.

5 'For her sins have reached to heaven, and God has remembered her iniquities.

6 'Render to her just as she rendered to you, and repay her double according to her works; in the cup which she has mixed, mix for her double.

7 'In the measure that she glorified herself and lived luxuriously, in the same measure give her torment and sorrow; for she says in her heart, 'I sit *as* queen, and am no widow, and will not see sorrow.'

8 'Therefore her plagues will come in one day — death and mourning and famine. And she will be utterly burned with fire, for strong *is* the Lord God who judges her.

9 'And the kings of the earth who committed fornication and lived luxuriously with her will weep and lament for her, when they see the smoke of her burning,

10 'standing at a distance for fear of her torment, saying, ''Alas, alas, that great city Babylon, that mighty city! For in one hour your judgment has come.''

11 'And the merchants of the earth will weep and mourn over her, for no one buys their merchandise any more:

12 'merchandise of gold and silver, precious stones and pearls, fine linen and purple, silk and scarlet, every kind of citron wood, every kind of object of ivory, every kind of object of most

head, and it will be the same in the future under the eighth.

14 '"These (the kings) will make war with the Lamb, and the Lamb will overcome them."'
16 '"And the ten horns . . . will hate the prostitute, make her desolate and naked . . . and burn her with fire."'

This is the about-face that occurs under the sixth plague when the waters of Babylon dry up. It becomes clear to the kings, that is to the national governments, that they have been deceived by being led to fight against God. The united Churches, mother and daughters, had persuaded them they would be serving God by enforcing a uniform religious practice. Now they see the matter differently. The result of this change of mind will be the utter ruin of civilization, as further described in Revelation 18:9-24. But before the prophet is shown that distressing picture, he hears messages of warning and entreaty that will enable some to escape.

ESCAPE! ESCAPE!

Revelation 18:1-8 'I saw another angel coming down from heaven, having great authority, and the earth was illuminated with his glory. And he cried mightily with a loud voice, saying, "Babylon the great is fallen . . . and has become the habitation of demons. . . . For all the nations have drunk of the wine . . . of her fornication . . . ." And I heard another voice from heaven saying, "Come out of her, my people, lest you share in her sins, and lest you receive of her

precious wood, bronze, iron, and marble;

13 'and cinnamon, and incense, fragrant oil and frankincense, wine and oil, fine flour and wheat, cattle and sheep, horses and chariots, and bodies and souls of men.

14 'And the fruit that your soul longed for has gone from you, and all the things which are rich and splendid have gone from you, and you shall find them no more at all.

15 'The merchants of these things, who became rich by her, will stand at a distance for fear of her torment, weeping and wailing,

16 'and saying, "Alas, alas, that great city that was clothed in fine linen, purple, and scarlet, and adorned with gold and precious stones and pearls!

17 "For in one hour such great riches came to nothing." And every shipowner, all who travel by ship, sailors, and as many as trade on the sea, stood at a distance

18 'and cried out when they saw the smoke of her burning, saying, "What *is* like this great city?"

19 'And they threw dust on their heads and cried out, weeping and wailing, and saying, "Alas, alas, that great city, in which all who had ships on the sea became rich by her wealth! For in one hour she is made desolate."

20 'Rejoice over her, O heaven, and *you* holy apostles and prophets, for God has avenged you on her!'

21 Then a mighty angel took up a stone like a great millstone and threw *it* into the sea, saying, 'Thus with violence the great city Babylon shall be thrown down, and shall not be found any more.

22 'The sound of harpists, musicians, flautists, and trumpeters shall not be heard in you any more. And no craftsman of any craft shall be found in you any more. And the sound of a millstone shall not be heard in you any more.

plagues. For her sins have reached to heaven . . . . And she will be utterly burned with fire, for strong is the Lord God who judges her." '

These powerful, world-wide messages, like the three messages in Revelation 14, must be proclaimed by human messengers. In declaring the fall of Babylon they will not be referring to her destruction under the plagues, for they are warning God's people who are still in Babylon to leave her lest they should suffer under the plagues. Therefore the fall of Babylon must refer to her moral and spiritual condition. The earlier announcement of the fall of Babylon in Revelation 14:8 has now been proclaimed for a century and a half. The spiritual condition of the Churches has grown much worse during this time. Biblical criticism has undermined faith in the Scriptures. The theory of evolution has removed creation and the Creator from the minds of many. The lovely doctrine of the love and grace of God has been presented in such a way as to do away with the law and justice of God. Overenthusiastic and emotional forms of worship have in many instances replaced serious study of the requirements of God and of any personal submission to them. Materialism has made men lovers of pleasure instead of lovers of God. The bereaved and ill are encouraged to seek solace

23 'And the light of a lamp shall not shine in you any more. And the voice of bridegroom and bride shall not be heard in you any more. For your merchants were the great men of the earth, for by your sorcery all the nations were deceived.

24 'And in her was found the blood of prophets and saints, and of all who were slain on the earth.'

19 After these things I heard a loud voice of a great multitude in heaven, saying, 'Alleluia! Salvation and glory and honour and power to the Lord our God!

2 'For true and righteous *are* his judgements, because he has judged the great prostitute who corrupted the earth with her fornication; and he has avenged on her the blood of his servants *shed* by her.'

3 Again they said, 'Alleluia! And her smoke rises up for ever and ever!'

4 And the twenty-four elders and the four living creatures fell down and worshipped God who sat on the throne, saying, 'Amen! Alleluia!'

5 Then a voice came from the throne, saying, 'Praise our God, all you his servants and those who fear him, both small and great!'

6 And I heard, as it were, the voice of a great multitude, as the sound of many waters and as the sound of mighty thunderings, saying, 'Alleluia! For the Lord God Omnipotent reigns!

7 'Let us be glad and rejoice and give him gory, for the marriage of the Lamb has come, and his wife has made herself ready.'

8 And to her it was granted to be arrayed in fine linen, clean and bright, for the fine linen represents the righteous acts of the saints.

9 Then he said to me, 'Write: "blessed *are* those who are called to the marriage supper of the Lamb!" ' And he said to me, 'These are the true sayings of God.'

10 And I fell at his feet to worship him.

from the spirits. It has become more important to make a name for oneself than to glorify God. Babylon's sins are reaching heaven. The hour of her destruction is approaching. There are many true worshippers of God in relapsed Churches. They must be urged to separate from Babylon while there is still time.

But he said to me, 'See *that you do* not *do that!* I am your fellow servant, and of your brethren who have the testimony of Jesus. Worship God! For the testimony of Jesus is the spirit of prophecy.'

THE UTTER RUIN OF BABYLON

9 *'"The kings of the earth who . . . lived luxuriously with her will weep and lament. . . when they see the smoke of her burning."'*
11 *'"And the merchants of the earth will weep and mourn over her, for no one buys their merchandise any more."'*
17 *'" "For in one hour such great riches came to nothing."'"*

In the Old Testament the prophets pictured the devil as the ruler of Babylon (Isa. 14:12-17), and they predicted her complete destruction: 'Against the king of Babylon . . . say: "How the oppressor has ceased, the golden city ceased." ' (Isa. 14:4.) ' "Babylon shall become a heap, a dwelling place for Jackals, an astonishment and a hissing, without an inhabitant." ' (Jer. 51:37.) The city of Tyre was also presented as ruled by the devil, and doomed to utter destruction. (Ezek. 28:12-19.) Our present prophecy does not mention Tyre by name, but presents a strikingly parallel picture of seafaring merchandise, as may be seen by comparing Revelation 18:11-17 with Ezekiel 27:3, 12-25. And of Tyre he predicted, ' " "I will make you like the top of a rock; you shall be a place for spreading nets, and you shall never be rebuilt." " ' (Ezek. 26:14.) The people of Tyre moved over to an island, and the ancient mainland city, like the ancient city of Babylon, has now been a desolate site for many centuries.

21-23 *'"Thus with violence the great city Babylon shall be thrown down, and shall not be found any more. The sound of . . . musicians . . . shall not be heard in you any more. And no craftsmen . . . shall be found in you any more. . . . For by your sorcery all the nations were deceived."'*

Thus the angel fills out the picture of the final effects of the plagues that will fall on one class of people. But before he finishes with this subject he gives us a glimpse of another group who have something to rejoice about.

A WEDDING CELEBRATION

Revelation 19:1-2 'I heard . . . a great multitude in heaven, saying, "Alleluia! . . . the Lord our God . . . has judged the great prostitute who corrupted the earth . . . .' '

7 ' "Let us be glad and rejoice and give him glory, for the marriage of the Lamb has come, and his wife has made herself ready." '

The restoration of ancient Jerusalem as the home of God's people was the heart burden of Isaiah, Jeremiah, Ezekiel, Daniel and Zechariah. Babylon was the oppressor of Jerusalem. The gaudily-arrayed prostitute, moved by the dragon, is the rival of the pure woman in celestial garments. When all contenders have been removed, the heavenly Bridegroom claims His bride, and His bride is the new Jerusalem. One of the plague angels came to John and invited him: ' "Come, I will show you the bride, the Lamb's wife," ' and John said, 'He showed me the great city, the holy Jerusalem, descending out of heaven from God.' (Rev. 21:9, 10.) God's people have been captive in mystic Babylon too long. The day of final deliverance is hastening towards us. The call to leave Babylon in heart and mind is urgent if we would enter into the glorious plans of God.

9 'Then he said to me, "Write: 'Blessed are those who are called to the marriage supper of the Lamb!' " '

The wedding itself, that is, the receiving of His kingdom, of which the new Jerusalem is the capital, takes place at the close of the preadvent judgement. (Dan. 7:13, 14.) As Jesus said to those who thought the kingdom was to appear immediately, ' "A certain nobleman went into a far country to receive for himself a kingdom and to return." ' (Luke 19:12.) And to His disciples He said, ' "And you yourselves be like men who wait for their master, when he will return from the wedding." ' (Luke 12:36.) ' "I bestow upon you a kingdom, just as my Father bestowed one upon me, that you may eat and drink at my table." ' (Luke 22:29, 30; Dan. 7:27.) What a celebration that will be! And when will it be fulfilled? When 'we who are alive and remain shall be caught up together with them (the resurrected ones) in the clouds to meet the Lord in the air. And thus we shall always be with the Lord.' (1 Thess. 4:17.)

THE CAPTURE OF THE BEAST, FALSE PROPHET AND DRAGON

The ten kings are to give their power and authority to the beast and together they make war on the Lamb. (Rev. 17:12-14.) The only way they can make war on the Lamb is by making war on the followers of the Lamb. They do so by supporting the false prophet in the decision that all who will not worship the beast are to be killed. (Rev. 13:14, 15.) In this way the kings of the whole world will be gathered to the battle of the great day. (Rev. 16:13, 14.) God's answer will come in the seventh plague when 'the fierceness of his wrath' will fall on this confederacy. (Rev. 16:19.)

11 'I saw heaven opened, and behold, a white horse. And he who sat on him was called Faithful and True, and in righteousness he judges and makes war.'

13 'He was clothed with a robe dipped in blood, and his name is called the Word of God.'

16 'And he has . . . a name written: King of kings and Lord of lords.'

He has other names too. This is Michael who, with his angels, fights against the dragon. (Rev. 12:7-9.) This is the Lamb whose wrath confronts the kings of the earth and drives them into hiding. (Rev. 6:15-17.) This is the Son of Man who causes all the tribes of the earth to mourn

11 Then I saw heaven opened, and behold, a white horse. And he who sat on him *was* called Faithful and True, and in righteousness he judges and makes war.

12 His eyes *were* like a flame of fire, and on his head *were* many crowns. He had a name written that no one knew except himself.

13 He *was* clothed with a robe dipped in blood, and his name is called the Word of God.

14 And the armies in heaven, clothed in fine linen, white and clean, followed him on white horses.

15 Now out of his mouth goes a sharp sword, that with it he should strike the nations. And he himself will rule them with a rod of iron. He himself treads the winepress of the fierceness and wrath of Almighty God.

16 And he has on *his* robe and on his thigh a name written:

KING OF KINGS
AND LORD OF LORDS.

17 Then I saw an angel standing in the sun; and he cried with a loud voice, saying to all the birds that fly in the midst of heaven, 'Come and gather together for the supper of the great God,

18 'that you may eat the flesh of kings, the flesh of captains, the flesh of mighty men, the flesh of horses and of those who sit on them, and the flesh of all *people*, free and slave, both small and great.'

19 And I saw the beast, the kings of the earth, and their armies, gathered together to make war against him who sat on the horse and against his army.

20 Then the beast was captured, and with him the false prophet who worked signs in his presence, by which he deceived those who received the mark of the beast and those who worshiped his image. These two were cast alive into the lake of fire burning with brimstone.

21 And the rest were killed with the sword which proceeded from the

when He appears on the clouds of heaven. (Matt. 24:30.) He is the Lord Jesus Christ who is to be 'revealed from heaven with his mighty angels in flaming fire' at His second advent. (2 Thess. 1:7, 8.)

19 'I saw the beast, the kings of the earth, and their armies, gathered together to make war against him that sat on the horse and against his army.'

14, 15 'The armies in heaven, clothed in fine line, white and clean, followed him on white horses. . . . out of his mouth goes a sharp sword, that with it he should strike the nations. . . . He himself treads the winepress of the fierceness and wrath of Almighty God.'

mouth of him who sat on the horse. And all the birds were filled with their flesh.

20 Then I saw an angel coming down from heaven, having the key to the bottomless pit and a great chain in his hand.
2 He laid hold of the dragon, that serpent of old, who is *the* Devil and Satan, and bound him for a thousand years;
3 and he cast him into the bottomless pit, and shut him up, and set a seal on him, so that he could deceive the nations no more till the thousand years were finished. But after these things he must be released for a little while.

It will take only the brilliance of His infinite holiness, and a mere word of command to destroy his enemies, as the apostle said: 'The lawless one will be revealed, whom the Lord will consume with the breath of his mouth and destroy with the brightness of his coming.' (2 Thess. 2:8.)

20 'Then the beast was captured, and with him the false prophet who worked signs in his presence, by which he deceived those who received the mark. . . . These two were cast alive into the lake of fire.'

Revelation 20:1-3 'An angel . . . laid hold of the dragon . . . and bound him for a thousand years . . . and shut him up . . . that he should deceive the nations no more till the thousand years were finished.'

The two great organizations known to us as the beast and the false prophet, who we have identified as the governments of the Vatican and the United States, simply disintegrate in the presence of the glorious Son of God. And the third power in this triumvirate, the dragon, who has been so active for so long, will be so confined that he will have nothing to do, and no companions except the evil angels whom he seduced into ruin. Can you imagine anything more uncomfortable to him than such confinement? But what of the ordinary people on the earth?

Revelation 19:21 'The rest were killed with the sword which proceeded from the mouth of him who sat on the horse. And all the birds were filled with their flesh.'

17, 18 'An angel . . . cried . . . to all the birds that fly in the midst of heaven, "Come . . . you may eat the flesh of kings . . . of captains . . . and . . . of all people, free and slave, both small and great.'

The battle of Armageddon is over. Opposition to God has collapsed. Persecuting organizations have disintegrated. Now there are only people on the earth, two classes of them, the persecuted and the persecutors. The Man of Many Names has a word of power to speak to each group. One group dies. The other hears Him call from the grave all those who have 'died in the Lord' and find themselves taken to heaven together with them. (Matt. 24:31; 1 Thess. 4:16-18.) And are we told what they will do there?

Many fanciful ideas about this period of a thousand years, popularly known as the millennium, are taught by earnest Bible students by bringing together verses of Scripture from many parts of the Bible. However, this one chapter, Revelation 20, is the only chapter in the whole Bible that mentions the millennium and speaks specifically about it. I urge the reader not to accept any teaching that does not conform to the plain statements in the verses we are now to consider.

COMPLETE VICTORY OVER SIN AND DEATH

Revelation 20:4-6 'I saw thrones, and they sat on them, and judgment was committed to them. And I saw the souls of those who had been beheaded for their witness to Jesus and for the word of God, who had not worshipped the beast or his image . . . they lived and reigned with Christ for a thousand years. . . . Blessed and holy

REVELATION 20

4 And I saw thrones, and they sat on them, and judgment was committed to them. And *I saw* the souls of those who had been beheaded for their witness to Jesus and for the word of God, who had not worshipped the beast or his image, and had not received *his* mark on their foreheads or on their hands. And they lived and reigned with Christ for a thousand years.

5 But the rest of the dead did not live again until the thousand years were finished. This *is* the first resurrection.

6 Blessed and holy *is* he who has part in the first resurrection. Over such the second death has no power, but they shall be priests of God and of Christ, and shall reign with him a thousand years.

7 Now when the thousand years have expired, Satan will be released from his prison

8 and will go out to deceive the nations which are in the four corners of the earth, Gog and Magog, to gather them together to battle, whose number *is* as the sand of the sea.

9 They went up on the breadth of the earth and surrounded the camp of the saints and the beloved city. And fire came down from God out of heaven and devoured them.

is he who has part in the first resurrection. Over such the second death has no power, but they shall be priests of God and of Christ, and shall reign with him a thousand years.'

So this will be the work assigned to those who have successfully resisted the deceptions of the devil. Their first official duties in heaven will be to serve as priests. '"The lips of a priest should keep knowledge, and people should seek the law from his mouth."' (Mal. 2:7.) Raised in the first resurrection will be those who like James were dispatched with a sword, and Paul who was beheaded. From among the living translated to heaven will be those who resisted the blandishments and threats of the authorities. This promised reversal of their situations should encourage those who suffer for the honour of their Lord. But these are not the only ones to serve as priestly judges. That will include all the 'blessed and holy'. (Verse 6.) The judgement committed to them must be the cases of the lost, and it will even include the fallen angels. (1 Cor. 6:2, 3.)

By allowing those to judge who have experienced the temptations and difficulties of this world, the Father is not merely turning the tables on those who formerly judged them. He is clearing His own name of any charge of arbitrariness in His dealings with the lost. And how will God's people be assigned to their work of judging? As the disciples will judge Israel (Luke 22:30), may not believers of other ages and racial groups be asked to assess the experience of their contemporaries among the lost? In this way many puzzling questions would be removed from their minds.

10 And the devil, who deceived them, was cast into the lake of fire and brimstone where the beast and the false prophet *are*. And they will be tormented day and night for ever and ever.

11 Then I saw a great white throne and him who sat on it, from whose face the earth and the heaven fled away. And there was found no place for them.

12 And I saw the dead, small and great, standing before God, and books were opened. And another book was opened, which is *the book* of life. And the dead were judged according to their works, by the things which were written in the books.

13 The sea gave up the dead who were in it, and death and Hades delivered up the dead who were in them. And they were judged, each one according to his work.

14 Then death and Hades were cast into the lake of fire. This is the second death.

15 And anyone not found written in the book of life was cast into the lake of fire.

7, 8 'When the thousand years have expired, Satan will be released from his prison and will go out to deceive the nations which are in the four corners of the earth.'

The resurrection of the vast multitudes of the lost of all ages (verse 5), will automatically release the devil from the confinement that prevented him from deceiving the nations. He immediately gets to work, and in his usual way — by deception.

8, 9 'To gather them together to battle . . . . They went up on the breadth of the earth and surrounded the camp of the saints and the beloved city.'

When John later on takes up the bright picture of the eternal home of the saved, he will explain how the holy city comes to be on the earth. (Rev. 21:2.) It does not come down empty. It is the dwelling place of the saints. Thus the devil persecutes the offspring of the woman to the very end. With God on their side there can be only one end to such a confrontation.

9, 10 'Fire came down from God out of heaven and devoured them. And the devil, who deceived them, was cast into the lake of fire . . . where the beast and false prophets are.'

The word 'are' has been supplied by the translators. The words 'were cast' would have been more suitable. The beast and the image were organizations made up of people. Faced with Almighty God, who to such is 'a consuming fire' (Heb. 12:29), the organization had disintegrated and the people had died and were left for the birds. Now the prophet says that the devil will have to face this same expression of the divine presence. But John has one more scene to show us before the fire comes down.

11, 12 'I saw a great white throne and him who sat on it . . . . I saw the dead, small and great, standing before God.'

If all the saved are in the city, and all the lost are mustered by the devil outside the city, the divine throne need only to appear above the city for all who have ever lived on the earth to feel summoned to judgement. And Satan with his angels are also there. A Hebrew prophet and a Christian apostle have both noted the words, '"I have sworn . . . that to me every knee shall bow."' (Isa. 45:23; Phil. 2:10.) Now is the moment for this to take place. In an earlier version John had already heard that submission made. He must have been viewing this very occasion when he recorded: 'Every creature which is in heaven and on the earth . . . all that are in them, I heard saying: "Blessing and honour and glory and power be to him who sits on the throne, and to the Lamb.'"' (Rev. 5:13.) Our Lord Jesus was sent not only to restore what Adam lost, but something vastly greater. 'In him (God chose) . . . to reconcile all things to himself . . . whether things on earth or things in heaven.' (Col. 1:19, 20.) What a beautiful picture of a divided universe united once again.

11 'Him who sat on it.'

He is not named. In the preadvent judgement it is the Ancient of Days who sits as judge, while the Son of Man is the advocate of His people. In the millennial judgement Christ and His people go over the records, seemingly for their own reassurance, for apparently no sentence follows. But in the Last Judgement, the One who sits on the throne must be the One who became one of us, for ' "the Father . . . has committed all judgement to the Son . . . and has given him authority to execute judgement also, because he is the Son of Man."' (John 5:22, 27.) 'We must all appear before the judgement seat of Christ.' (2 Cor. 5:10.)

12 'And books were opened. And another book was opened, which is the book of life. And the dead were judged according to their works, by the things which were written in the books.'

I am glad that it is not only from the records kept by the angels that we shall be judged. (Eccles. 5:6.) Only if we are judged from the Lamb's book of life is there any hope. (Col. 1:27; Rev. 3:5; 21:27.)

14, 15 'Then death and Hades were cast into the lake of fire. This is the second death. And anyone not found written in the book of life was cast into the lake of fire.'
10 'And they will be tormented day and night for ever and ever.'

For the meaning of 'forever' in this connection, see the note on Revelation 14:11. The lake of fire is to be the death of death, so it cannot be an eternal process of dying. But when all over the earth fire comes down from God upon those raised in the second resurrection, and upon the devil and his angels, the whole surface of the planet would become an extensive sea of flame in which all the pollution that sin has caused will be destroyed. (Mal. 4:1; 2 Peter 3:10.) Thus the way is prepared for the bright picture that yet remains for us to consider.

The events of the millennium

LAST DAYS

FIRST RESURRECTION
Return of Jesus
Righteous dead raised
Living saints taken up
Wicked slain
Satan bound
Earth desolated

THOUSAND YEARS
Righteous in heaven
Wicked remain dead
Satan bound by chain
of circumstances
Earth at rest

SECOND RESURRECTION
Christ, saints and city descend
Wicked dead raised
Satan loosed
Last judgement
Satan and sinners destroyed
Earth cleansed and renewed

ETERNITY

REVIEW

1 Do all the previous symbols of those who misuse political or religious power come together in this further prediction of their destruction?

2 Does this chapter explain how Euphrates will be dried up? How will it be done?

3 How was John informed that the papal head and the ten kings were still future in his day?

4 How was it made clear that the things shown in this further vision still lay further ahead?

5 What are some of the corruptions that have already spoiled the spiritual purity of the daughter churches of Babylon?

6 What shows God's concern for those of His people who are still in Babylon? Should we be concerned about them?

7 When Christ appears to complete the war of Armageddon, when the seventh plague has done its work, what disposition will He make of those who have been led by the dragon?

8 What temporary disposition of the dragon himself will be made?

9 Of what value to any human being would be his participation in the judgement that takes place during the millennium?

10 What event will free Satan from his imprisonment, and how will he make one last revelation of his true character?

11 When Satan and his supporters have surrounded the holy city what do they face before they are destroyed?

12 Will Satan acknowledge the justice of God before he is destroyed? Why is this important?

9 The eternal kingdom of God

We have called this chapter 'The Eternal Kingdom of God' because it is the reality presented to king Nebuchadnezzar when a Stone struck his metal image of human history — '"a kingdom which shall never be destroyed"' to be set up by '"the God of heaven"'. (Dan. 2:34, 44.) But we may also call it 'The Eternal Home of the Saved', for Jesus said, '"Seek the kingdom of God, and all these things shall be added to you. Do not fear, little flock, for it is your Father's good pleasure to give you the kingdom."' (Luke 12:31, 32.)

Revelation 21:1 'I saw a new heaven and a new earth, for the first heaven and the first earth had passed away. Also there was no more sea.'

The Lord originally created the earth to be inhabited. (Isa. 45:18; Gen. 1:28.) Ever since the Flood, two-thirds of the surface of the planet has been covered with water or ice. Now it has been cleansed by fire the original plan can be carried out. Restored to its early condition and climate, there will be plenty of room for the saved to possess it.

THE HOLY CITY

2 'Then I, John, saw the holy city,

REVELATION 21 and 22

21 And I saw a new heaven and a new earth, for the first heaven and the first earth had passed away. Also there was no more sea.

2 Then I, John, saw the holy city, new Jerusalem, coming down out of heaven from God, prepared as a bride adorned for her husband.

3 And I heard a loud voice from heaven saying, 'Behold, the tabernacle of God *is* with men, and he will dwell with them, and they shall be his people, and God himself will be with them *and be* their God.

4 'And God will wipe away every tear from their eyes; there shall be no more death, nor sorrow, nor crying; and there shall be no more pain, for the former things have passed away.'

5 Then he who sat on the throne said, 'Behold, I make all things new.' And he said to me, 'Write, for these words are true and faithful.'

6 And he said to me, 'It is done! I am the Alpha and the Omega, the Beginning and the End. I will give of the fountain of the water of life freely to him who thirsts.

7 'He who overcomes shall inherit all things, and I will be his God and he shall be my son.

8 'But the cowardly, unbelieving, abominable, murderers, sexually immoral, sorcerers, idolaters, and all liars shall have their part in the lake which burns with fire and brimstone, which is the second death.'

9 Then one of the seven angels who had the seven bowls filled with the seven last plagues came to me and talked with me, saying, 'Come, I will show you the bride, the Lamb's wife.'

10 And he carried me away in the Spirit

new Jerusalem, coming down out of heaven . . . prepared as a bride.'

Jesus said He was going to prepare a place for His followers. (John 14:1-3.) And here it is, the city God has prepared for those who embrace His promises and confess that they are but pilgrims in the present life. (Heb. 11:13-16.)

3-6 '"God himself will be with them and be their God. . . . There shall be no more death, nor sorrow, nor crying . . . no more pain, for the former things are passed away." . . . And he said to me, "Write, for the words are true and faithful . . . . I will give of the fountain of the water of life freely to him who thirsts."'

Yes, unbelievable as it may seem. No more pain. No more dying. And best of all, God will not seem far away.

7-9 '"He who overcomes shall inherit all things . . . . But the cowardly, unbelieving, abominable, murderers, sexually immoral, sorcerers, idolaters, and all liars shall have their part in the lake that burns with fire . . . the second death."'

It is these things that have brought pain and sorrow. But why include the unbelieving? Because there is no other way to be saved. The way of salvation is not a human invention. It is a plan in which God took our griefs, sorrows, and sins upon Himself. There are none righteous. (Rom. 3:10.) '"He who

to a great and high mountain, and showed me the great city, the holy Jerusalem, descending out of heaven from God,

11 having the glory of God. And her light *was* like a most precious stone, like a jasper stone, clear as crystal.

12 Also she had a great and high wall with twelve gates, and twelve angels at the gates, and names written on them, which are *the names* of the twelve tribes of the children of Israel:

13 three gates on the east, three gates on the north, three gates on the south, and three gates on the west.

14 Now the wall of the city had twelve foundations, and on them were the names of the twelve apostles of the Lamb.

15 And he who talked with me had a gold reed to measure the city, its gates, and its wall.

16 And the city is laid out as a square, and its length is as great as its breadth. And he measured the city with the reed: twelve thousand furlongs. Its length, breadth, and height are equal.

17 Then he measured its wall: one hundred *and* forty-four cubits, *according* to the measure of a man, that is, of an angel.

18 And the construction of its wall was of jasper; and the city *was* pure gold, like clear glass.

19 And the foundations of the wall of the city *were* adorned with all kinds of precious stones: the first foundation *was* jasper, the second sapphire, the third chalcedony, the fourth emerald,

20 the fifth sardonyx, the sixth sardius, the seventh chrysolite, the eighth beryl, the ninth topaz, the tenth chrysoprase, the eleventh jacinth, and the twelfth amethyst.

21 And the twelve gates *were* twelve pearls: each individual gate was of one pearl. And the street of the city *was* pure gold, like transparent glass.

22 But I saw no temple in it, for the Lord God Almighty and the Lamb are its temple.

23 And the city had no need of the sun or of the moon to shine in it, for the

does not believe is condemned already."' (John 3:18.) 'God has given us eternal life . . . in his Son. He who has the Son has life.' '"Whoever believes in him should not perish but have everlasting life."' (1 John 5:11, 12; John 3:16.)

9-12 'One of the seven angels . . . . showed me the great city, the holy Jerusalem . . . having the glory of God. . . . She had a great high wall with twelve gates, and twelve angels at the gates, and names written on them . . . the names of the twelve tribes.'

Do you belong to the tribes of Israel? 'The book of the genealogy of Jesus Christ, the son of David, the son of Abraham.' (Matt. 1:1.) 'By faith Abraham obeyed when he was called to go out to the place which he would . . . receive as an inheritance. And he went out, not knowing where he was going. By faith he sojourned in the land of promise as in a foreign country . . . for he waited for a city which has foundations, whose builder and maker is God.' (Heb. 11:8-10.) 'As many of you as were baptized into Christ have put on Christ. . . . And if you are Christ's, then you are Abraham's seed, and heirs according to the promise.' (Gal. 3:27-29.)

14-17 'The wall of the city had twelve foundations, and on them were the names of the twelve apostles . . . . the

glory of God illuminated it, and the Lamb *is* its light.

24 And the nations of those who are saved shall walk in its light, and the kings of the earth bring their glory and honour into it.

25 Its gates shall not be shut at all by day (there shall be no night there).

26 And they shall bring the glory and the honour of the nations into it.

27 But there shall by no means enter it anything that defiles, or causes an abomination or a lie, but only those who are written in the Lamb's book of life.

22 And he showed me a pure river of *the* water of life, clear as crystal, proceeding from the throne of God and of the Lamb.

2 In the middle of its street, and on either side of the river, *was* the tree of life, which bore twelve fruits, each *tree* yielding its fruit every month. And the leaves of the tree *were* for the healing of the nations.

3 And there shall be no more curse, but the throne of God and of the Lamb shall be in it, and his servants shall serve him.

4 They shall see his face, and his name *shall be* on their foreheads.

5 And there shall be no night there: They need no lamp nor light of the sun, for the Lord God gives them light. And they shall reign for ever and ever.

6 Then he said to me, 'These words *are* faithful and true.' And the Lord God of the holy prophets sent his angel to show his servants the things which must shortly take place.

7 'Behold, I am coming quickly! Blessed *is* he who keeps the words of the prophecy of this book.'

8 Now I, John, saw and heard these things. And when I heard and saw, I fell down to worship before the feet of the angel who showed me these things.

9 Then he said to me, 'See *that you do* not *do that*. For I am your fellow servant, and of your brethren the prophets, and of those who keep the words of this book. Worship God.'

city is laid out as a square, and its length is as great as its breadth. . . . the city . . . twelve thousand furlongs . . . . its wall: one hundred and forty-four cubits.'

What a size! Three hundred and seventy-five miles on each side! Would even England and Wales fit into it? Plenty of room, and how brilliant its appearance!

18-21 'The construction of its walls was of jasper; and the city was pure gold . . . . And the foundations . . . all kinds of precious stones . . . . each individual gate was of one pearl. And the street . . . pure gold.'

No dust. No grime. No reinforced cement. No need for street lighting. Listen —

22-26 'I saw no temple in it . . . . the glory of God illuminated it . . . . and the kings of the earth bring their glory and honour into it. . . . (there shall be no night there).'

What a brilliant picture! God is not hidden in a temple. He dwells with His people. What could the kings of earth add to it? Perhaps the prophet speaks of those he had described earlier as having been 'made . . . kings and priests to . . . God', those whose sins had been washed in blood. (Rev. 1:5, 6.) This agrees with his next words.

27 'There shall by no means enter it anything that defiles . . . but only those who are written in the Lamb's book of life.'

As Peter put it, 'We . . . look for

10 And he said to me, 'Do not seal the words of the prophecy of this book, for the time is at hand.

11 'He who is unjust, let him be unjust still; he who is filthy, let him be filthy still; he who is righteous, let him be righteous still; he who is holy, let him be holy still.'

12 'And behold, I am coming quickly, and my reward *is* with me, to give to every one according to his work.

13 'I am the Alpha and the Omega, *the* Beginning and *the* End, the First and the Last.'

14 Blessed *are* those who do his commandments, that they may have the right to the tree of life, and may enter through the gates into the city.

15 But outside *are* dogs and sorcerers and sexually immoral and murderers and idolaters, and whoever loves and practises a lie.

16 'I, Jesus, have sent my angel to testify to you these things in the churches. I am the Root and the Offspring of David, the Bright and Morning Star.'

17 And the Spirit and the bride say, 'Come!' And let him who hears say, 'Come!' And let him who thirsts come. And whoever desires, let him take the water of life freely.

18 For I testify to everyone who hears the words of the prophecy of this book: If anyone adds to these things, God will add to him the plagues that are written in this book;

19 and if anyone takes away from the words of the book of this prophecy, God shall take away his part from the book of life, from the holy city, and *from* the things which are written in this book.

20 He who testifies to these things says, 'Surely I am coming quickly.' Amen, Even so, come, Lord Jesus!

21 The grace of our Lord Jesus Christ *be* with you all. Amen.

new heavens and a new earth in which righteousness dwells.' (2 Peter 3:13.)

Revelation 22:1-3 'And he showed me a pure river of the water of life . . . proceeding from the throne of God . . . . and on either side of the river, was the tree of life . . . yielding its fruit every month. And the leaves . . . for the healing of the nations. And there shall be no more curse.'

Our first parents lost the tree that would perpetuate life when they sinned. Blessed loss! Now the tree is restored. The Garden of Eden is now set in the centre of the city like a city park. And what wonderful herbal remedies are supplied! Healing leaves and plenty of fruit.

3, 4 'The throne of God and of the Lamb shall be in it . . . . They shall see his face, and his name shall be on their foreheads.'

Perhaps the last thought is the most important — we shall be like Him, for we shall be able to see Him. (1 John 3:2.) Is it just possible that this planet, where the Son of God adopted human nature to bring us back to our allegiance, would become the new centre of the universe? Over and over God has offered to dwell with His people and be their God. The majority have been lovers of pleasure more than lovers of God. But for those who cherished their daily walk with God, like Enoch, it will become a literal reality.

WILL YOU BE THERE?

6-9 'He said to me, "These words are faithful and true." . . . And when I heard and saw, I fell down to worship before the feet of the angel who showed me these things. . . . He said to me . . . "Do not do that . . . Worship God." '

This is the second time John had been overcome with reverence for the angel who through him has sent this whole revelation to us. (Rev. 1:1; 19:10.) It is the second time that the angel of prophecy has explained that the important thing is not the messenger but the message and the One who sends it. It is the second time also that he mentions those who keep the words of this book. Will this include you?

11, 12 ' "He who is unjust, let him be unjust still; he who is filthy, let him be filthy still; he who is righteous, let him be righteous still; he who is holy, let him be holy still. . . . Behold, I am coming . . . and my reward is with me." '

Placed together like this, these two statements seem to be

reminders that before the coming of our Saviour the decree of the Ancient of Days will have been given. It is up to us to ensure that it will be in our favour.

14, 15 'Blessed are those who do his commandments, that they may have the right to the tree of life, and may enter through the gates into the city. But outside are dogs and sorcerers and sexually immoral and murderers and idolaters, and whoever loves and practises a lie.'

The ten commandments were given to Israel when God accepted them as His people. (Exod. 19:3, 5; 20:3-17.) The angel has twice before placed an emphasis on the keeping of the commandments. (Rev. 12:17; 14:12.) Now again the commandments are emphasized by first a positive statement and then a negative statement. In the list of sinners in our text, dogs may seem out of place, but this term was used to describe active homosexuals, as may be seen from the parallelism in Deuteronomy 23:17, 18. Christianity is more than a creed. It is a living, personal experience. It is cherishing Jesus' words of instruction and letting them control our ideals and actions. It is finding in Christ's way that fullness of joy that makes the pleasures and amusements of the world seem insipid. It is discovering that 'he who has the Son has life'. (1 John 5:12.) Jesus' own invitation to us is recorded at the close of His Revelation.

16-21 '"I Jesus, have sent my angel to testify to you these things . . ." the Spirit and the bride say, "Come!" . . . He who testifies to these things says, "surely I am coming quickly."'

Does the holy city, the bride of the Lamb, have more attraction for you than the transient pleasures of this world? Does the Holy Spirit seek to draw you to have faith? Will all that Jesus has done to deliver us from evil be of no avail for you, or will you accept it? The power to save and keep you is His. The decision to accept His offer and remain united to Him is yours.

When Jesus ascended after His crucifixion, and appeared in heaven for us as 'a Lamb with the marks of sacrifice' upon Him, those who were present at the throne were moved to sing a song of praise. This outburst was immediately followed by the voices of myriads of angels in a sevenfold acclamation: '"Worthy is the Lamb who was slain to receive power and riches and wisdom, and strength and honour and glory and blessing!''' (Rev. 5:6, 9-12.) In a sevenfold, that is, a perfect gift, nothing is held back. Is not this the response that should flow from our hearts and lives when we think of Him?

REVIEW

1 What evidence have you that there will be room enough on the renewed earth for the multitudes of the redeemed to live?

2 What to you will be the greatest attraction of the holy city and new earth?

3 How may we prepare ourselves to enjoy what God has prepared for them that love Him?

BIBLIOGRAPHY

Anderson, R. A., *Unfolding Daniel's Prophecies.*

Anderson, R. A., *Unfolding the Revelation.*

Maxwell, C. M., *God Cares*, vol. 1, Daniel, vol. 2, Revelation.

Smith, U., *Daniel and Revelation*.

SDA Bible Commentary, Commentary on Daniel and Revelation.